MOUNT AND MOUNTAIN
VOLUME 1

A REVEREND AND A RABBI
TALK ABOUT THE TEN COMMANDMENTS

Smyth & Helwys Publishing, Inc.
6316 Peake Road
Macon, Georgia 31210-3960
1-800-747-3016
©2012 by Rami Shapiro and Michael Smith
All rights reserved.
Printed in the United States of America.

The paper used in this publication meets the minimum requirements of
American National Standard for Information Sciences—
Permanence of Paper for Printed Library Materials.
ANSI Z39.48–1984. (alk. paper)

Library of Congress Cataloging-in-Publication Data

Shapiro, Rami M.
Mount and mountain / by Rami Shapiro, Michael Smith.
volumes cm
ISBN 978-1-57312-612-0 (alk. paper)
1. Ten commandments--Criticism, interpretation, etc. I. Smith, Michael, 1954 Sept. 1- II. Title.
BV4655.S49 2012
222'.1606--dc23

2011048498

MOUNT
and
MOUNTAIN

VOLUME 1

A Reverend and a Rabbi Talk About
the Ten Commandments

Michael Smith *and* Rami Shapiro

Also by Rami Shapiro and Michael Smith

Let Us Break Bread Together: A Passover Haggadah for Christians

Dedication

To everyone with the faith and courage to engage
the Word anew. —RS

To E. Glenn Hinson, who taught me the value of
cross-tradition conversation. —MS

Contents

PREFACE   1

EDITOR'S NOTE   3

A NOTE ON THE TRANSLATION   5

First Thoughts: An Introduction   7

Chapter 1: First Commandment (Exodus 20:2)   15

Chapter 2: Second Commandment (Exodus 20:3-6)   23

Chapter 3: Third Commandment (Exodus 20:7)   35

Chapter 4: Fourth Commandment (Exodus 20:8-11)   45

Chapter 5: Fifth Commandment (Exodus 20:12   57

Chapter 6: Sixth Commandment (Exodus 20:13)   68

Chapter 7: Seventh Commandment (Exodus 20:13)   79

Chapter 8: Eighth Commandment (Exodus 20:13)   97

Chapter 9: Ninth Commandment (Exodus 20:13)   107

Chapter 10: Tenth Commandment (Exodus 20:14)   115

Conclusion   127

BIBLIOGRAPHY   133

Preface

Here's the story: a minister and a rabbi start a blog. Sure, it sounds like the opening of a joke, a twenty-first-century update, perhaps, on the slew of moth-eaten, hand-me-down rabbi, priest, and minister gags whose punch lines we all know by heart. But it isn't. In this particular case, it happens to be the truth. In 2008, Baptist minister Reverend Michael Smith, PhD, and Jewish rabbi Rami M. Shapiro, PhD, did indeed start a virtual conversation via blogspot.com. Called "Mount and Mountain," a reference to Mount Sinai, on the one hand, and the Galilean hill called Mount Eremos, on the other, the blog recorded a long-running, serialized dialogue between Mike and Rami in which the pair interpreted, argued about, and interrogated two key texts drawn from the canons of their respective religions: the Ten Commandments from the Torah, and the Sermon on the Mount from the Gospel of St. Matthew.

This book represents the first half of Mike and Rami's dialogue, focused on the Ten Commandments. In it, Mike and Rami discuss the nature of divinity, the power of faith, the beauty of myth and story, the necessity of doubt, the achievements, failings, and future of religion, and, above all, the struggle to live ethically and in harmony with the way of God. They do not, thank goodness, always agree. Nor, thank goodness, do they fall to bickering or polemic. Rather, they talk—openly, honestly, passionately, speaking from a place of deep conviction; not a conviction, by the way, that either one of them is *right*, but that it is through inquiry, through questioning, and through exploration that truth comes to light.

And it seems to me that this is the real strength of their conversation: not their respective certainties, but their shared trust in *not knowing* and their shared effort of seeking knowledge by talking together. Theirs is a wild, wandering conversation, branching off into unexpected directions, rambling into unfamiliar territories, twining itself into strange and fascinating shapes like kudzu climbing streetlamps and telephone poles along the side of a highway. This is because, as with the best conversations, neither Mike nor Rami have any stake in where the conversation is going. They aren't headed anywhere. They have no foregone conclusions. What they do have is a belief that, in opening the Scripture and reading it together, something new will emerge, something that neither could discover on their own.

Here, we have a model of a different kind of interfaith dialogue that neither preaches nor placates but challenges its participants to work both singly and together in the task of reinterpreting sacred texts. Neither resolution nor consensus is the goal of this book. It settles nothing. Rather, it is open-ended, stirring up possibilities and inviting its readers to parse those possibilities for themselves. Reading along, we are invited to *take part*, to add our own voices and experience to the task of interpretation, and to wrestle side by side with Mike and Rami, to craft our own meanings from the text of Exodus. And if, as readers, we take that text in our own directions, each of us nevertheless always moves toward a richer understanding not only of Scripture but also of God and godliness.

What this book brings home, then, is that sacred texts are never really *finished*—an important point in a time when zero-sum, exclusivist religions seem to be gaining ground. Instead, they are living things, changing and growing as they pass through history, and also as they pass between readers, each of whom must renew the Scripture in his or her own way, for his or her own life. Indeed, as readers and interpreters of Scripture, we are not unlike Mr. Charlton Heston, who, in Cecil B. DeMille's famous film *The Ten Commandments*, found himself playing the roles of both God and Moses. We too are doubly cast. We stand on the mountaintop awaiting the word of God, and though the voice we eventually hear cannot be other than our own, reciting its lines aloud, it may yet return to us transformed, made resonant by an encounter with the Divine.

This book aspires to such an encounter. Happy reading.

Aaron Herschel Shapiro

Editor's Note

I have been involved in this conversation since its inception. I read, along with many others, each blog entry as it was posted, and I regularly commented on what these two teachers were saying. When asked to edit the series and tasked with turning two years of dialogue into two volumes of text, I admit to being both honored, overwhelmed, and a bit intimidated. The blogs had their own integrity and their own limitations. Sometimes offline conversations between Rami and Mike allowed them to make assumptions about one another's positions that the blog reader could not make or follow. Sometimes their friendship steered them into byways of little or no interest to the general reader. It fell upon me to eliminate the extraneous, clarify the essential, and help the reader engage these two thinkers with the same depth and informality with which they engaged each other. Add to this the fact that Rami is my father, and you have some sense of how challenging this job was to me. I want to thank both Mike and my father for the opportunity to work on this project. And I want to make it clear to the readers that while I am responsible for the overall readability of this book, the ideas expressed here belong entirely to its authors, Mike and Rami. This is their conversation. Yet my hope is that, reading through the dialogue, one will be drawn (as I have been) to add one's own voice to the din, to follow Mike and Rami's example and talk back to the text. That, in the end, is what a great conversation is all about: it compels us to join in.

Aaron Herschel Shapiro

A Note on the Translation

One of things we ought to clarify from the beginning is the numbering of the Ten Commandments. While all versions of the *Aseret HaDibrot* (The Ten Words), as the Ten Commandments are called in Judaism, are based on Exodus 20:2-17 and its variant in Deuteronomy 5:6-18, there are different ways of listing them.

In Judaism, Exodus 20:2 is the First Commandment, whereas it's considered a preface in Christianity. Judaism then links verses 2 through 6 together to make the Second Commandment. Most Protestants, with the notable exception of Lutherans, consider either verse 3 by itself or combine verses 2 and 3 as the First Commandment. Roman Catholics and Lutherans take verses 2-6 to be the First Commandment and then divide verse 17 into two parts so that 17a, "You shall not covet your neighbor's house," becomes the Ninth Commandment and 17b, "You shall not covet your neighbors wife," becomes the Tenth.

For the purposes of this book, we have decided to work with the numbering system of the Jews, primarily because it is the oldest of the existing systems. Additionally, it should be noted that a number of variant translations of the Ten Commandments are available. While most translations are similar, there are nevertheless significant differences that arise and that often allow for, or demand, different interpretations. Therefore, in the interests of increasing our interpretive range, we have decided to use both all and none of them. The translation that appears here, as well as below the chapter headings, and that provides the primary basis for our discussion is an original one written by Rabbi Rami Shapiro specifically for this project. However, throughout the text we will also refer to the JPS, NIV, and KJV translations whenever these variants allow for unique and/or valuable alternate readings.

—RS & MS

First Thoughts: An Introduction

Rami: Before we get into the actual text of the Ten Commandments, it might be helpful to both of us, and to those who are reading this conversation, to know where each of us is coming from regarding religion, as well as where we stand regarding the Bible.

I was born into a first-generation American Orthodox Jewish family. My parents were thoroughly New World, my grandparents primarily Old World. The tension natural to this kind of situation revolves around honoring the old in the context of the new. For many Jews of my parents' generation, this meant joining the Conservative wing of American Judaism, something my parents and their entire community did when I was fourteen years old. But my spiritual formation took place in an Orthodox setting. I did and do keep kosher, observe the Sabbath and holy days, and study Torah daily. Of course it helps to have a job that requires this, but I suspect I would do it regardless.

As I grew into my own spiritually, I left Conservative Judaism for more liberal settings. Orthodoxy seeks to replicate as much as possible the Judaism of the Talmud. Conservative Judaism still places Talmudic teachings and practice at its core, but tends to be more open to the social mores of American egalitarianism and democracy. Reform Judaism, through which I received my first rabbinic ordination, focuses less on rabbinic dictates and more on prophetic social action and calls for justice and compassion. Upon receiving my ordination in 1981, I lead a congregation aligned with the Reconstructionist movement. Reconstructionism seeks to blend the Conservative movement's honoring of tradition with Reform's call for social action. Nine years later, I received my second rabbinic ordination from Rabbi Zalman Schachter-Shalomi, my rebbe or spiritual master, along with the title Rebbe, making me a part of his spiritual lineage that focuses on the Hasidic and mystic side of Jewish teaching and practice. Either I am very eclectic or very confused. Or both.

Simultaneous with my work within Judaism, I pursued religious studies outside of Judaism. I no longer believe that any religion captures the fullness of human religious creativity or truth. Instead, I believe that only by studying multiple religions can we begin to approximate an understanding of the spiritual dimension of reality. The more I delved into Buddhism, Hinduism, Taoism, and the mystical schools of Christianity and Islam, the more similarities I noticed. While I do not believe all religions are true, or that all religions are saying the same thing, I do believe that the mystic geniuses of all religions (and none) experience the same truth—the absolute nonduality of all things in, with, and as God. Of course, calling that truth "God" already reflects my Western bias, and I am not wedded to the word. Indeed, I have long since abandoned the notion that language can capture reality. As the Taoist sage Lao Tzu puts it in the opening line of the *Tao Te Ching*, "The Tao that can be named is not the Eternal Tao."

So, if you'll pardon a tree analogy, I am a liberal mystic whose roots are in the unknown and unknowable, whose trunk is Jewish and is devoted to the wisdom of the Hebrew Bible, and whose branches reach into the mystical and contemplative traditions of the world's religions in order to derive nourishment from truth as it is manifest both in the light above and in the dark soil below.

Given this, I have nothing to defend. That is to say, in our dialogue I look forward to articulating my understanding of Judaism without the burden of having to defend it as the one true faith. That is a belief I do not carry. Judaism is just one expression of human religiosity, and, for me, no expression is complete. So there will be no debate here, but rather honest inquiry. I want to share what I think, learn from what you think, and, where what you think is more compelling to me than what I think, to change what I think. In short I want to learn more than teach. And, since I know this is your desire as well, this conversation will be far richer than either of us can imagine at this point.

Now since our conversation is focused on the Bible, let me share some of my thoughts on the Bible. For me, the Bible is a human document. It is not so much God's revelation to humanity as it is humanity's quest for God and godliness. Because the Bible is a human document, it reflects the best and the worst of our capabilities. When it reflects the best, I believe the author is in touch with God and revealing godliness by speaking in what I call the Voice of Love. When it reflects the worst, I believe the author is out of touch with God and speaking to the needs of ego in what I call the Voice of Fear. When reading the Bible, we must identify which Voice we are hearing. When we hear the Voice of Love, we should do our best to follow its advice. When we hear the Voice of Fear, we should own that shadow side of our personality but refuse to act on its commands.

For example, when the Bible says "Love your neighbor as yourself" (Lev 19:18) or "Love the stranger" (Lev 19:34), it is speaking in the Voice of Love, and we would be wise to heed its wisdom. However, when the same Bible commands us to massacre every man, woman, child, and cow of Amalek (1 Sam 15:1-2), it is speaking in the Voice of Fear, and we must recognize our human capacity for genocide even as we renounce all acts of genocide.

Saying this raises the question, "What is God?" I imagine we will deal with that when we get to the first of the Ten Commandments, but suffice it to say that I believe God is Reality. God is the One Thing from which and in which all things arise and fall. In this I follow the Apostle Paul who says that it is in God that we live, move, and have our being (Acts 17:28). You and I and all things are manifestations of the One Thing called God.

Given this notion of God, I understand God's commands as analogous to an ocean's current or to the grain of wood. If you wish to be in harmony with the ocean you move with the current. If you wish to cut wood well, you cut with the grain. You can move against the current and cut against the grain, but in the end this will prove ineffective.

The Voice of Love reveals the grain of God or the current of godliness. If you want to live well, if you want to live in harmony with Life and the One who manifests it, this is the way to live. What are the consequences for violating these commands? Needless suffering, confusion, pain, anger, greed, ignorance, and violence both for yourself and for the world as a whole.

So rather than read these commandments as the barkings of a Cosmic Drill Sergeant, I understand them as challenges. The Ten Commandments challenge us to live in harmony with the current of godliness rather than in subjugation to the demands of an aloof and dictatorial god.

Mike: Where do I come from with regard to religion, and what do I think about the Bible and God?

I was born among Southern Baptists and Cumberland Presbyterians, some active and some lapsed. My four grandparents, in particular, influenced me in key ways through their love for the stories of the Bible, their practical approach to applying Scriptures to daily life, and their insistence that one think for oneself.

Books played a large role in my early spiritual formation. Fiction, history, biography, and science were my favorite subjects. Even as I tried to prepare for a career in science, writers such as Tolkien and Lewis caught my attention. Lewis introduced me not only to his particular approach to Christianity but also to a wide range of other writers. Looking back, I now see that these various writers set up a kind of ongoing conversation within me with regard to God, creation, humanity, Scripture, the church, science, and my own place or role in what many Christian thinkers label "God's economy." As a result, I've come to value honest conversation with others, including (or perhaps especially) those whose experience or perspective is different from my own.

The religion faculty at Belmont College taught me the basic methodologies of biblical and historical studies. More important, I think, they convinced me of the possibility that both my heart and mind could find a home in Christianity. E. Glenn Hinson nurtured my love for church history, introduced me to masters of Christian spirituality, encouraged the independent development of my personal gifts, and modeled responsible interfaith conversation. My debt to Glenn is great, and I hope our conversation serves as partial payment.

I am an ecumenical Baptist Christian. As such, I treasure the contributions of the multiple branches of Christianity even as I continue to practice the faith from within my particular tradition. In addition, I believe God loves the world and that all creation, to some extent, reveals God. I, therefore, pay attention to the great world religions, seeking to understand their origins and development, core teachings and practices, relationships to other religions, and potential connections with my own faith tradition. The best hope for peace and justice in the world may lie in nurturing friendships across religious boundaries and in the conversations that occur in the context of such friendships. Let's dare to hope our conversation may serve as a model.

As for my approach to the Bible, first let me say that I believe the Bible is a human/divine book. Christians generally believe the Holy Spirit inspired and guided its various authors, so that whatever they produced may be used to turn us to God. Scripture's deepest purpose, therefore, is to help God form us into his kind of people. Scripture is a tool in God's hands. Christians must take care never to confuse the tool with God, lest they turn the Bible into an idol.

Second, I believe the Bible must be interpreted and applied. This implies the need for some standard or standards of interpretation. Some Christian groups look primarily to the teaching tradition of the church. Others vest considerable authority in church structures, such as councils of bishops.

Those in the free-church tradition tend to give enormous weight to individual interpretation, tempered by interaction with other believers. Many prefer to attempt to interpret Scripture in light of Scripture.

Personally, I attempt to interpret all of Scripture in light of what we know of Jesus. Matthew, Mark, Luke, and John are my primary texts, my canon within the canon. Focusing on these texts enables me to disregard Scriptures that clearly violate the teaching and spirit of Jesus. Stoning disobedient children, slaughtering conquered people, vengeance, and the like go by the wayside. They do not pass the Jesus test.

As for God, I find him best revealed in Jesus. In Jesus, we see who God is and what he does, at least to the extent possible for mortals. The God revealed is one who takes a highly personal, love-driven interest in all creation, including us. He takes risks—selecting and shaping a group of former slaves into his people, becoming one of us in the Incarnation, entrusting his work in the world to all-too-fallible humans. He chooses to limit himself lest he overwhelm us and compel our allegiance, for he will settle for nothing less than our voluntary love.

The Ten Commandments, then, are best seen as God's vision for his people, individually and collectively. Grappling with them and, even more, trying to put them into practice push our spiritual development. Through them God says, "This is the kind of life I created you to have and the kind of life you can have. This is my kind of life. Join me in living it."

Rami: I understand that Christians believe that the Holy Spirit inspires the Bible, but that doesn't tell me what you believe. Officially, Jews believe that God dictated the Torah to Moses on Mount Sinai, but I don't believe that. So, if you believe the Bible is inspired by the Holy Spirit, I would like to know that, and how you think that worked.

I am also wondering about your personal standard of interpreting the Bible in light of Jesus. Given all the conflicting studies on the life and teaching of Jesus, I suspect that Jesus has become a Rorschach blot where we project the Jesus we want into the text. So I need to know who you think Jesus is before I can understand your standard.

And then there is the problem of using the canonical Gospels. Is the Jesus of Matthew, say, the same as the Jesus of John? And, given what we know about the evolution of the Gospels and how they have changed over time, can you really trust them? There is also the question of discounting the noncanonical gospels, especially the Gospel of Thomas and even the hypothetical Q Gospel. As a pastor, you may have to limit yourself to the Official Text on Sunday, but as a scholar you are not so constrained.

In a sense, we are both wrestling with the same problem: what to do with all the violence and hate in the Hebrew and Greek Bibles. I understand and envy your ability to dismiss the violence in the Hebrew Bible by assuming that Jesus would reject the violent God who visits such destruction on humanity. I do the same thing when I say these texts reflect the Voice of Fear. But I suspect that you have a problem that my more humanistic approach avoids.

Because I claim the Bible is a human document, I can explain the Bible's violence, misogyny, homophobia, etc. as reflecting the mores of its time. I can note these as historical artifacts and ignore them as ethical or moral guidelines for the present. But if I argue, as you seem to do, that the Holy Spirit inspired these texts, I have to ask "Why?" Why teach me about Noah and a god willing to destroy almost all life on earth, when the real God would never do that? Or would he?

If Jesus is your standard, you have to deal with the Little Apocalypse in Mark 13. Jesus says, "In those days there will be suffering, such as has not been from the beginning of the creation that God created until now, no, and never will be" (Mark 13:19). So Jesus' God is as mad as Noah's. And then there is the book of Revelation that paints a picture of Jesus himself as a bloodthirsty warrior. If the Holy Spirit inspired these teachings, then the mad God of the Hebrew Bible is still wreaking havoc in the New Testament.

So help me out here. If Jesus is your standard, paint me a picture of this Jesus and show me how you manage to escape the other images of him that don't fit your picture.

Mike: Perhaps I misconstrued your point (not an uncommon occurrence when communicating via print). I thought you wanted us to share the perspective each of us would bring to the task of dealing with the biblical text, specifically the Ten Commandments. This is only fair; with regard to our readers, they now have an opportunity to evaluate our individual conclusions in light of our stated assumptions.

It seems to me the first two posts accomplished the goal. Unpacking, evaluating, and even refining our assumptions in an extended preface is beyond the scope of our current task. I'll not deny it might be great fun, even intellectually stimulating, yet remain in the end a diversion from the main job.

I suggest we move on and start to deal with particular texts. That will be quite enough of a task for one book. Other biblical texts are best reserved for our next project!

Our perspectives, then, will interact as we deal with particulars rather than generalities. No doubt, we'll be drawn into debates from time to time, resolving some and leaving others standing, subject to the judgment of our readers. We might even change one another's minds on occasion.

That being said, I'll provide a summary response to some of your questions and concerns.

1. God inspired the writers, but God never overrode their humanity. In practical terms, this means all scriptural accounts reflect the culture, language, politics, economics, science, ethical perspective(s), etc. of the author's day. To put it quaintly, God seems to have been willing to run the risk of collaborating with fully human authors, accepting the inevitable dangers of such a relationship. To put it theologically, God refused the benefits of straight dictation in favor of preserving human freedom. The result is mixed. God shines clearly through in some texts, less so in others, and scarcely at all in many places.

2. When it comes to the Bible, I choose (there's really no other way to put it) to operate within the confines of the canon. That's my scholarly and faith-based position. A significant number of biblical scholars from the last third of the twentieth century take a similar position. Essentially, the approach accepts the results of the process of canonization and focuses energy on interpreting and applying the Bible to the life of the church.

3. The danger of Jesus becoming a kind of Rorschach blot is very real; it always has been for that matter. Knowing a bit of the history of interpretation may help us guard against this tendency but cannot entirely remove it. Still, some disciplines, such as interpreting Jesus' actions and words in the context of first-century theological, political, and sociological currents may help us avoid the worst excesses.

4. I do not distinguish between the God of the Old and New Testaments. The role of particular stories in each, though, may change when interpreted in light of Jesus. Stories that may once have been thought prescriptive now become warnings to the people of God: "Once you thought this was what God wanted you to do or think—you got it wrong—remember the story, and never forget."

It should be interesting to see how or if our different starting places actually influence interpretation.

The Ten Commandments (Exodus 20:2-14)

1. I am YHVH Your God, who brought you out of the land of Egypt, out of the house of bondage. (Exodus 20:2)

2. You shall have no other gods before Me. You shall not make for yourself any graven image, nor any manner of likeness, of any thing that is heaven above, or that is in the earth beneath, or that is in the water under the earth. You shall not bow down to them, nor serve them, for I, YHVH Your God, am a jealous God, visiting the iniquity of the fathers upon the children unto the third and fourth generation. (Exodus 20:3-6)

3. You shall not take the Name of YHVH Your God in vain; for YHVH will not hold him guiltless that takes His Name in vain. (Exodus 20:7)

4. Remember the Sabbath, to keep it holy. Six days you shall labor, and do all your work; but the seventh day is a Sabbath unto YHVH Your God, in it you shall not do any manner of work, you, nor your son, nor your daughter, nor your man-servant, nor your maid-servant, nor your cattle, nor the stranger that is within your gates; for in six days YHVH made heaven and earth, the sea, and all that in them is, and rested on the seventh day. Wherefore YHVH blessed the Sabbath day, and made it holy. (Exodus 20:8-11)

5. Honor your father and your mother, that your days may be long upon the land which YHVH God gives you. (Exodus 20:12)

6. You shall not murder. (Exodus 20:13)

7. You shall not commit adultery. (Exodus 20:13)

8. You shall not steal. (Exodus 20:13)

9. You shall not bear false witness against your neighbor. (Exodus 20:13)

10. You shall not covet your neighbor's house, nor his wife, his manservant, his maidservant, nor his ox, nor his ass, nor anything that is your neighbor's. (Exodus 20:14)

First Commandment

I am YHVH Your God, Who brought you out of the land of Egypt, out of the house of bondage. (Exodus 20:2)

Rami: To understand the deeper meaning of this first of the Ten Commandments, I want to explore the meaning of two Hebrew words, YHVH, the name of God, and Eretz Mitzrayim, the Land of Egypt. Most English Bibles translate YHVH as "Lord," following the rabbinic custom of replacing the name YHVH, which cannot be pronounced, with the euphemism Adonai, or Lord, which can be pronounced. The problem is that using Adonai or Lord gives us a picture of God that is quite at odds with the original YHVH. Notions of God as king and lord promote a patriarchal, hierarchical, and military bias that has more to do with the political structure of the time the text was written (or translated) than it does with the nature of God. YHVH, while used as a proper noun in the Hebrew Bible, is actually a form of the Hebrew verb "to be." Torah tells us quite clearly that God is a verb, a process, and not a static being or even the Supreme Being.

This is made all the more clear at the burning bush (Exod 3:14) when Moses asks God's name, which is to say when Moses asks God to reveal the true nature of divinity. God replies, "*Ehyeh asher Ehyeh,*" mistakenly translated as "I am that I am." The translation "I am" implies that God is static, fixed, and unchanging, whereas *Ehyeh* literally means "I will be," revealing God as dynamic, fluid, and ever changing. God cannot be fixed in form or concept. In other words, whatever your theology, the only thing you can be certain of is God is not that.

The Hindus have a wonderful Sanskrit phrase for this concept: *neti neti,* "not this, not that." Whatever you think God is—God isn't. God cannot be reduced to ideas about God. Which of course leads us to the Second Commandment regarding idols. But let's wait on that for a moment and continue with our current text.

Reverend and a Rabbi Talk about the Ten Commandments

In the First Commandment, God says, "I am the unfixed, the unconditioned, and the unconditional. I am the always becoming; I am change. I brought you out of *Eretz Mitzrayim*."

I am using the Hebrew here to uncover a meaning that is lost on readers of standard English translations of the Bible where *Eretz Mitzrayim* is usually translated as "the land of Egypt." In fact, *Eretz Mitzrayim* is a pun in Hebrew that means "the narrow places." The First Commandment defines God as the unconditional and creative process whose primary purpose, at least from the Jewish perspective, is to liberate us from slaveries of all kinds. God not only liberated us from Egypt in the past; God frees us from the narrow places of our lives in the present. God is the power that liberates us from the bondage of certainty, fixed forms, fixed ideas, etc., but only if we have enough faith in God not to define God. The First Commandment, then, as I understand it, expresses the challenge of *neti neti*: it calls us to free ourselves from all ideas about God that we might experience the liberating power of God.

Mike: Exodus 20:2 sets the overarching parameter within which all following verses should be interpreted—namely, the kind of God who is dealing with the Israelites.

Your point about *YHVH* dovetails nicely with a long-standing Christian insight: God, the creator of space-time, transcends space-time. God has no past or future; God dwells in an eternal present. For God, all moments are the moment at hand. If nothing else, the verse drives home how different God is from us or from anything in our experience. God indeed is wholly other. The commandment does not call us to handle God carefully; it asserts that God is beyond all handling.

All of which raises a question: how might we possibly know such a God? The answer lies in the phrase "Who brought you out of Egypt, out of the land of slavery."

God transcends space-time, but he may choose to operate within it. After all, it is his creation. While the Israelites (or we, for that matter) must never fall into the trap of believing that God can be fully understood, neither are they (or we) left adrift without a hint as to the nature of God. They are to look to what God has done in a specific portion of space-time: the actions of God that combine to make what we may call "the exodus event."

We learn something about God by pondering what God does. What might the ancient people of God have learned from the exodus event?

1. *God's penchant for acting in history.* The God of the exodus is not an absentee divinity or even a present but disengaged one. This God gets his hands dirty, working in the history of real people. He starts not with a final product but with the materials to hand, in this case a people mired in the actuality and mentality of slavery. If ever they are tempted to act as if their God is indifferent or disconnected, let them remember the exodus. God makes history the arena in which we most often meet and start to know him.

2. *God's determination to eradicate the slave mentality.* He has taken them from "the narrow places" into a wide-open wilderness. All kinds of possibilities are now open to them. It's exhilarating. It's frightening. That's how life is going to be for God's free people. Whatever else we may say, God is in the liberation business. Let those who would enslave others beware. Just as important, let his people beware of falling back into any form of slavery.

So God has chosen to make history significant for his people. He will act in history to reveal himself to them, potentially freeing them from false concepts of God and of themselves and thereby forming them into a new kind of people. The commandments that follow continue God's formation work.

Rami: I want to comment on your notion that God is "wholly other." If you mean that God is wholly other than anything we can conceive, then I agree. This is again the Hindu teaching of *neti neti:* not this, not that. But if you mean to say that God is wholly separate, then I disagree.

I am a panentheist (*pan*/all, *en*/in, *theos*/god), a nondualist. For me, all reality rests in God, as God. This is how I understand the Hebrew term *HaMakom*, "the Place," one of the names of God in the rabbinic tradition. God is the place in which all life happens. God is the field out of which the universe grows, in which it lives, and to which it returns. Or, if you prefer, God is that "in which we live and move and have our being" (Acts 17:28). God is both immanent and incarnate as the world and yet transcendent in that God is greater than the world.

I most often use the Hindu metaphor of the ocean and wave to get this idea across. The ocean represents God, and the waves represent creation. Just as each wave is unique and distinct, and yet not other than the ocean that manifests it, so each of us—all things—are unique and distinct and yet not other than God. And, just as an ocean is more than the sum of its waves, so God includes and transcends the sum of creation.

While I am certain you grasp what I am saying, I am pretty certain you see things differently, and that difference will come up for us over and over again.

I love your phrase "God is beyond all handling" and, as you imply, God is beyond all knowing as well. As Lao Tzu writes in the opening verse of the Chinese *Tao Te Ching*, "The Tao that can be named is not the Eternal Tao." Again, *neti neti*, any god we can imagine is not the Eternal God. There is a similar sentiment in Exodus 33:22, where we learn that God cannot be seen face to face. This means we cannot know God fully or directly because the god we would know would be a creature of our imagining, an idol. But while we can't know the entirety of God's being, we can nevertheless learn from God a *way* of being. This is what Lao Tzu calls the *te*, the way of Tao as we humans come to know it when we act in harmony with it. It is the *te* of God that is revealed to Moses: mercy, grace, patience, overflowing love, abundant trustworthiness, and forgiveness (Exod 34:6).

So how does God act in the world? I would suggest that God doesn't act *in* the world, but rather *as* the world. Again, this is what I mean by God incarnate as nature—the ocean manifest as wave. Nature is God's body, the divine incarnate as the myriad forms and processes of the natural world. When we deeply and truly understand that body, which includes our bodies, we discover its *te*. And, if we choose to act in harmony with God's *te*, we liberate others and ourselves from tyrannies of all kinds.

I see the exodus as parable rather than history. God, Moses, Pharaoh, etc. are aspects of myself. Pharaoh is my tendency to enslave and be enslaved; God is my capacity to end that slavery; and Moses is the means by which I can do so. If I follow the *te* of God, the way of mercy, grace, forgiveness, etc., I can free myself from bondage and end the bondage in which I have enslaved others.

This is God acting in history not as "other" but as you and me. This is why the story requires human agents: Shifra and Puah, the midwives; Yochabed and Miriam, Moses' mother and sister; Pharaoh's daughter and Zipporah, Moses' wife; and Moses himself. Each of these people tapped into and lived the *te* of God, and in so doing brought liberation closer to reality. God doesn't intervene in history, but godliness unfolds in history.

Mike: "Wholly other" means God is beyond our grasp, greater than anything we can conceive. Insofar as I can tell, we agree.

I am not a panentheist. Were I not a Christian, I probably would be. At least two factors keep me from taking the step. First, both Testaments stress that we must not confuse God with the creation. God may be glimpsed and even experienced through creation, but he is more than, even other than, his creation. Creation is sacred but not divine. Second, the incarnation pushes me to say God is known best through personality and relationship (as opposed to through creation per se or a sacred text). So I think you are probably right. We differ on this matter.

That being true, I find it interesting that we arrive at similar conclusions. Take your point about the *te*. In place of "the way of Tao," I probably would say "the way of Christ" or "the way of God" or "the way of the Holy Spirit." As we come to know what can be known of God, and insofar as we act in harmony with what we know, we become partners with God in the world. Mercy, grace, patience, overflowing love, forgiveness, and the like are the traits and tasks of such partners.

We start from different places with regard to the exodus. I see exodus as history (at long distance), which may be interpreted as parable or allegory. Paying attention to history, though, sets limits on the range of possible interpretations. I would have no problem asking, "What does the story of Miriam say to us about our own hearts?" The answer is that Miriam's story reveals our complexity, that strange blend of love, ambition, pettiness, and nobility found within each of us. It also reveals that, even so, we may still become partners with God as he reshapes humanity and the world.

Rami: I understand your hesitation about panentheism, though I find the statement "were I not a Christian, I probably would be [a panentheist]" to be quite interesting.

I won't belabor the point, but are you saying that if you didn't know better as a Christian you would be fooled into taking the next best but still false position of panentheism? Or are you saying that because you are a Christian you cannot accept panentheism even though you suspect it's true?

I ask this because I wrestle with this kind of thing all the time. As a Jew, there is much I am supposed to accept that as a thinking postmodern human being I cannot accept. I have rejected such notions as Chosen People, Israel as the Holy Land, and the exclusivity of God's revelation in the Hebrew Scripture. I let truth (as I understand it) trump tradition every time. I suspect you do as well, but you may be better at making room for truth in your tradition than I am in mine. To be blunt, I am tired of making Judaism say things that I believe to be true but that the classical Jewish sages would reject. I would rather just say what I believe to be true and let Judaism fend for itself.

Okay, on to something else.

I, too, am surprised (pleasantly) that while we seem to start from different places, we end up with similar positions. I say "seem to start" because there is much less to our differences than our word choices might suggest.

While I call the exodus a parable and you call it history, we both approach the text as story and ask the same question: What does the story mean to us today? Whether we call the text history or parable matters less than how we use it, and because we use it more as a guide to psycho-spiritual truth than historical fact, we come to some very similar conclusions.

Given your statements about panentheism and Taoism, let me suggest two books that you might find interesting. You may have read these already, but they were new to me. The first is Sallie McFague's *The Body of God*, which argues that panentheism represents the fullest understanding of Christian incarnationalism. The second is *Christ the Eternal Tao* by Hieromonk Damascene, which reveals the deep affinity between Taoism and the teachings of Jesus.

Mike: I want to add a little more to our conversation about panentheism and Christianity.

I wrote that were I not a Christian I might well be a panentheist. You mention two possible interpretations of my meaning. I had a third in mind: I choose Christianity because I find it persuasive in light of incarnation, the story of God's interactions with the ancient people of God and the church, and in light of my personal experience. Panentheism seems to me to be the great "other option." If Christianity is not "true" (and we probably need to spend some time defining the term "truth"), panentheism is the next most likely candidate. It seems possible to me that a key insight of panentheism (God is in all and all rests in God) may be subsumed within a Christian understanding of reality.

Christianity, over the course of its history, has cast a rather wide net. To my way of thinking, the Christian tradition provides room enough in which to think carefully and assimilate insights from any era, even the emerging era (whatever that may come to mean).

Our discussion about panentheism aside, we may certainly say that "story" is our meeting ground, at least so far. God speaks creation into existence; the Word becomes flesh. The power of story—to make something new, to reveal what has been hidden, to provoke bone-deep change in a person or a community, to reveal what may be known of God—is close to the heart of Christianity. It is also the link between Christianity and other religions, insofar as I can tell. When in doubt, lay aside other matters, and listen to the story. Imagination may well be God's surest path to one's deepest self.

Rami: I love the fact that you introduce the idea of story here, and raising it along with the question of what constitutes truth is vital.

A central function of the ego is to take the facts of its existence and weave them into a narrative that provides it with purpose and meaning. A story is "true" in so far as it provides purpose and meaning, and "false" if it does not.

Obviously, "true" and "false" in this context are necessarily subjective. Christianity is true for you in that it provides you with a compelling narrative that gives purpose and meaning to your life. Other religions are less true, or perhaps even false, in that their respective narratives are personally less compelling, purposeful, and meaningful. I would rather stay away from notions of "true" and "false" and focus instead on the impact of religious belief on the life of the believer. My criteria for judging the efficacy of a religious position is the extent to which that position moves the believer to greater and greater levels of compassion and justice.

In my own case, there is no single compelling religious narrative. There are parts of many religions that I find meaningful and that provide me with purpose, and I sew these together in a patchwork narrative that speaks to me, because it challenges me to live a life of ever-increasing compassion and justice. The thread that holds my quilt together is panentheism, the notion that God is both the source and substance of all reality.

The value of story is its gift of myth and metaphor. When you note that God speaks creation into being, I assume you take this figuratively. God doesn't "speak" the way you and I do, but there is something about the nature of speech that lent itself as a metaphor to the mystery the author of this passage was trying to articulate. Our job is not to defend a flat literalism that insists God has vocal cords and speaks Hebrew; our job is to explore the nature of speech to see what meaning we can glean from the metaphor.

For me, the giving of the Ten Commandments is a story. The question I ask is not "did it happen as the Torah says" but "what meaning can I find in the story itself." In this we are in perfect agreement: "lay aside other matters, and listen to the story. Imagination may well be God's surest path to one's deepest self."

Second Commandment

You shall have no other gods before Me. You shall not make for yourself any graven image, nor any manner of likeness, of any thing that is heaven above, or that is in the earth beneath, or that is in the water under the earth. You shall not bow down to them, nor serve them, for I, YHVH Your God, am a jealous God, visiting the iniquity of the fathers upon the children unto the third and fourth generation. (Exodus 20:3-6)

Rami: Before we get into the details of this commandment, I want to offer a general comment on how I understand the entire notion of "You shall not."

As you know, I don't believe in a self-conscious god who stands apart from the universe and directs things. I believe that God and the universe are one; again, to use the Hindu metaphor, the universe is God the way a wave is the ocean. So the image of a commanding God is not compelling, and I take it to reflect the limits of the author's imagination rather than any truth about God. I believe that the author of this commandment discovered something very profound but could only express it in the language of command. To get at that discovery, I find the work of Orthodox Christian theologian Jean-Yves Leloup quite helpful. According to Leloup, we should freely translate "You shall not" as "You are capable of living without," and in this way make all the more clear that, as the First Commandment said, it is the very nature of God to call us toward liberation.

Following Leloup, the Second Commandment says, "You can live without any image of God whatsoever. You can stand in direct relation to What Is and not get misled by ideas about What Is. When you stand alone, free from idols, creeds, dogmas, and beliefs, you stand in direct relation to That Which Is."

To be with God without idols and images is to be surrendered of self. The "I" and the "thou" are both surrendered to the infinite One Who Is All. This is what happens during meditation. As I sit in silence, the "I" that sits is silenced as well. There is no "me" sitting at all. When the "I" returns, when my egoic mind reappears, it does so lighter than before. It no longer holds as tightly to the idolatry of self. But, lightly held or not, there is still idolatry. That is to say, when the ego returns, it brings its images of God with it.

What I need to do is remind myself that these idols are not God, but only ego-projected images of God. The key is not to live without idols, but never to mistake the idol for God. Look at that opening line again: "You shall have no other gods before Me." Why does Torah say "before Me"? Why not just say, "You shall have no other gods"?

The reason is this: When we are before God, i.e., in the *presence* of God, we are surrendered into the One Who Is All; there is no "I" to recognize anything, and there are no idols to be recognized. This is like a person who shines a penlight outside in the bright noonday sun. The light is on, but you cannot see it; you cannot recognize it as separate from the greater light of the sun. When I stand in the light of God, both "I" and all things become transparent; both "I" and all things are revealed to be God, the One and Only Thing.

But I don't always live in the noonday light of God. Sometimes I imagine myself to be in the shadows, and there my penlight works just fine. In the darkness, the lesser lights of humanity's pantheon of gods and goddesses may be useful, but only if we realize they are the Named and not the Eternal Tao; that is, they are images of God, not God. So when I am in the dark, I have no problem calling out to Jesus, Krishna, Ganesh, Allah, Yah, Durga, Kuan Yin, or any other image of God and using that image to spread a little light. I just don't want to cling to that image when the darkness has passed and I stand again in the noonday brightness of God.

There is much more to say about this, and about what it means that God is jealous and visits the sins of the fathers upon the children, but let me stop here and get your take on things.

Mike: I agree the commandment requires a great deal of unpacking. I'll stick with verses 3-4 in this installment.

The first thing that strikes me is the magnitude of the task God sets himself. He intends to wean the Israelites from the normative religious assumption of the day: polytheism. To put it another way, God sets out to teach them the discipline (or art) of monotheism.

Step 1 in this long process is to lead the people to unlearn an old habit and practice a new one. Your translation of "before God" as "in God's presence," Rami, captures the idea: "You shall not recognize the gods of others in My presence." Since God is present with his people always, this amounts to saying, "Now that I am with you, you must stop treating other gods as God."

The commandment does not address the people's feelings. They may well go on feeling as if other gods are real, that those gods have powers potentially useful or dangerous, and that a wise person prefers not to offend them.

God starts with actions. This nearly always surprises us. Yet any competent spiritual director recognizes the formation technique. For example, we learn to pray not by mastering a theory of prayer but by praying, often using patterns created by others.

Changing metaphors, we learn to play a piano by practicing set finger techniques. Music theory comes later, if at all. Imagine the Israelites in the wilderness as would-be pianists of varied talent, all of whom have had their potential corrupted by exposure only to the technique available in the ancient Egyptian music scene. God must wean them from this technique in order to teach them how to make his kind of music.

In the commandment, God establishes a new practice routine for his people-in-the-making. They will find it hard going. When I was young, I took piano lessons. Many a time, I skipped or shortened practice in order to go and do something I already knew how to do (read a book, play baseball, watch television). In short, while my idols or gods were fairly petty, they still had quite a grip on me. So it was for the Israelites, and so it is for us in our time. The second portion of the commandment begins to address this problem.

Rami: Here's an odd thought: What if polytheism is better suited to our times than monotheism?

Monotheism isn't just the belief in one abstract godhead; rather, each monotheistic religion believes that its idea of God is the one true idea of God. The inherent exclusivity of monotheism makes it competitive and even violent, and thus, as Constantine realized, a far better tool for empire building than polytheism, which, by allowing for the legitimacy of many gods and ideas about God, has no need to defeat other gods or impose one homogeneous religious system.

Monotheists do better in a homogeneous world, but the twenty-first century is far from homogeneous, and it may be that polytheists are better suited to navigating the plethora of gods, truths, and realities that make up our postmodern global village than monotheists will ever be.

Abrahamic monotheists try to get around this problem through what might be called the "Abrahamic fiction": the idea that Jews, Christians, and Muslims worship the same God. Again, God, as we humans understand God, always exists within a theological frame. In this context, the word we use for God refers simply to our ideas and claims about God; and the theological claims of Judaism, Christianity, and Islam are mutually incompatible. If any one of these religions is true, the other two are false.

The only way to prove which religion is true is global jihad. By definition, the true God always wins. Since this is inconvenient to say the least, most of us postpone this war to the mythic future, though all too many of us are currently working to make that future a reality here and now.

Polytheism doesn't have this problem. Live and let live, believe and let believe, is its creed. This is much more suited to life in the global village than monotheism's begrudging "you're wrong and you're damned, but I won't kill you; I'll let God deal with you later."

So, whereas the Second Commandment may have been a practical tool for consolidating the diverse Jewish tribes and their gods, it may be the wrong policy for our time. Perhaps we need a different revelation: "You shall recognize all gods as Me, for I am infinite and cannot be reduced to one form or idea or religion or theology. I manifest as all form even as I transcend all form." Or, as the 4,000-year-old *Rig Veda* of the Hindus puts it, *Ekam Sat Viprah Bahuda Vadanti*: "Truth is one. Different people call it by different names."

Mike: Let's start with what I think is an error in your analysis of polytheism and monotheism: the assumption that both approaches are concerned with ideas about God.

From the outside looking in, it may appear that way. I suspect, though, that throughout history's long course most polytheists—not the philosophers, perhaps, but the everyday followers—have believed their particular god(s) to be quite real. For example, a Norseman making sacrifice to Thor did not think of Thor as an idea but as a red-haired, hammer-wielding, belt-wearing god who could provide tangible assistance. Ancient fertility gods attracted worshipers not because they represented the annual renewal of nature but because people thought they were real beings that might ensure a harvest or bring about the birth of a child.

Similarly, monotheists by and large do not worship an idea of God. Instead, they believe they are called to devote themselves to the One God. The majority of monotheists throughout history have assumed God to be actively concerned for the creation, for the people he has drawn to himself, and for the rest of humanity as well.

I think you would suggest that in both cases the gods or God worshiped are constructs of the human mind. My personal position is "yes and no." God reveals himself in any number of ways. I think he most fully reveals himself through the story of a particular people with roots deep in Middle Eastern history and through the "ripples" that spread out from that history. Such a God is beyond packaging. At the same time, no one can deny our tendency to attempt to package God in ways amenable to our cultures, sub-cultures, professional disciplines, or personal tastes. Unfortunately, some of these packages amount to little more than tribalism written large—hence religious wars and persecution.

All of which leads me back to the matter of idols. After all, what is an idol other than a religious package of some sort? The Second Commandment, and monotheism itself (at its best), points to the God who transcends all our packages.

Rami: You raise an excellent point: I am indeed speaking of religion from the outside, and I'm doing so consciously and as clearly as I can. Whenever we speak about something, we are, by definition and necessity, standing "out-side" of it.

And, since I believe God is not an object from which one can stand apart, God is not something one can speak about. So, again, I am back to Lao Tzu, "The tao that can be named is not the Eternal Tao." Any god we can name, define, and cram into a theology is not the Eternal God, or what Meister Eckhart calls the "Godhead." We cannot talk about the Eternal God, we can only deal with our ideas about this God, no matter how strongly we insist we are doing otherwise.

For me, then, your position that the living God reveals himself most fully through the story of the Jews is not verifiable outside the claim itself. The fact that the Jewish Bible says the Jews are God's chosen is no more convincing than the fact that the Gospels claim Jesus is the Son of God. What else would they say? Sacred texts are held sacred by the people who benefit from calling them sacred. There is no way around this.

Like you, I, too, am wary of tribalism, but all religion, in so far as it promotes in-groups and out-groups—chosen and not chosen, saved and damned, believers and infidels—is tribal. Yet tribalism in and of itself need not always lead to conflict and war.

I think war is inevitable when tribalism embraces a zero-sum worldview: salvation is restricted to the few who do God's will as the tribe defines it. Tribes within a polytheistic frame do not have this zero-sum problem. The gods of Canaan were not at war with the gods of its neighbors. War came with the Hebrews and their zero-sum god who commanded them to destroy the Canaanite gods and those devoted to them.

I also agree that the Second Commandment insists we abandon our religious packages for God, but I would then say, given the ineffable nature of the Godhead, all religiously packaged gods are idols reflecting the imagination and bias of their inventors. For me, the Second Commandment argues for radical humility when it comes to both religion and the idols that the adherents of one or another religion imagine and worship.

Saying all this does not, however, mean that all gods and religions are equal. As I wrote earlier, I rank the quality of religions and gods by one criterion: the extent to which they bring people to an ever-deepening commitment to justice and compassion for all beings.

Mike: You said, "I rank the quality of religions and gods by one criteria: the extent to which they bring people to an ever-deepening commitment to justice and compassion for all beings." I might add "humility" to the list, but otherwise we agree.

I, of course, speak from within a religious tradition. My particular tradition (Christianity with a Protestant and Baptist flavor) includes self-correctives to zero-sum tribalism. Two examples come to mind: the parable of the good Samaritan and the parable of the sheep and goats. Both challenge self-interest and tribalism. I suspect the commandments perform a similar function. The Sermon on the Mount does as well. The tragedy is that Christians seldom give themselves wholly to such visions.

Obviously, my operating assumption that God reveals himself most fully through the story of the Jews and Jesus is not verifiable. It is a faith assumption, a postulate if you will. I've found the postulate works for me. It leads me to confront my own self-centeredness, xenophobic tribalism, and the systems that encourage such things. Speaking personally, it has also led me to experience a sense of the presence of God, sometimes strongly, sometimes less so.

Once again, though, I'm struck by how our different starting points seem to lead us to similar conclusions about what is important. Take your point about needing a "radical humility" when it comes to understanding religions (both our own and those of others). I agree with you. We also agree about the desired end result of good religion: justice and compassion. I suspect both of us think good religion aims at authentic community building, though I might say this is God's vision for humanity, while you might argue it's inherent in reality.

Perhaps my tradition has something to contribute at this point: radical religious freedom. Baptist Christians, with some notable recent exceptions in the United States, have always insisted on religious liberty. By this we mean that government has no rightful role to play in support of any religion. Instead, each individual is free to choose or reject religion of any kind. Religious freedom is an inherent right. It should not be confused with religious tolerance, which assumes some group has authority to give or withhold permission. Put into practice, religious freedom functions as a partial antidote to zero-sum thinking.

Of course, all of the above is costly in that it often sets one in opposition to perceived self-interest or cultural norms. Spiritual formation, I think, always requires that we die in some sense in order to live an authentic human life.

Rami: Just when I was hoping for a good ol' knock-down-drag-out fight, it turns out we agree again. Maybe we need to bring in a shill.

Anyway, I agree that humility is the sign of an authentic person of faith. I know my story is just a finger pointing to the moon (as the Zen people say) and never the moon itself. No story is verifiable. That is what Gödel's incompleteness theorem tells us. What Kurt Gödel said in 1931 about mathematical systems is true for all philosophical and theological systems: they rest on un-testable assumptions. That is why the value of a religion rests not on the rightness of its theology but on the effects of its beliefs on its believers. By their fruits you shall know them. Works may not get you into heaven, but they certainly matter here on Earth.

I am intrigued that your faith has led you "to experience a sense of the presence of God." My own experience is the opposite. I love the story in Exodus 22:25. God is instructing Moses on how to build the Ark of the Covenant. One expects God to meet Moses in the Ark, and then God says He will meet Moses "above the cover, from between the two cherubim that are on top of the Ark." In other words, God will meet Moses outside the box! Literally. That is true in my experience. I never find God in the box of religion, but only when the box is stripped away; it is only when I stand in a place of unknowing that I experience the *Shekhinah*, the presence of God.

I know what you are saying regarding radical religious freedom and the Baptist faith. I imagine most people would be surprised to learn that it was Virginia Baptists who helped elect James Madison to Congress, and did so largely on his promise to fight for religious freedom and the First Amendment. But that was a long time ago. Today, the Baptist brand or, to be more accurate, the Southern Baptist brand is often associated with forces opposing the very religious freedoms it once supported. How sadly ironic.

Your last remark, "spiritual formation, I think, always requires that we die in some sense in order to live an authentic human life," is also fascinating. While this may not pertain directly to our topic, it is too rich a comment to let slip by. The Sufis have a saying, "Die before you die," and I am certain we can find similar statements in most religions.

The way I understand this is dying to my story, dying to the box that I might stand outside of it and meet God. What dies is my egoistic, or better, my narcissistic tendency to see myself reflected in my images of God and truth. I would love to hear a little more from you about your sense of dying.

Mike: Let's take the issues you raise one at a time.

1. You wrote, "I am intrigued that your faith has led you 'to experience a sense of the presence of God.' . . . I never find God in the box of religion, but only when the box is stripped away . . . ." Start with the "box." The longer I live with Christianity, the more liberating it becomes. The God who meets me within Christianity keeps pushing at the boundaries. The "box" keeps getting bigger and bigger.

Like you, I find it interesting that liberation has come to us in different ways. Perhaps this has to do with our starting places. While born into a culture dominated by Christianity, I found my early spiritual home in literature and science. God sought and found me there in the stories associated with various mythologies, the novels of writers such as Lewis and Tolkien, the simple basics of physics and astronomy and the like. I backed into Christianity through such things. As a result, Christianity is not so much a box as a universe in which God becomes ever more real to me.

As for the presence of God, my personal experience is modest. All I can really say is that at various moments I've known in my bones that I'm standing on holy ground in the presence of God, the One revealed in Jesus yet also the One beyond knowing. On the basis of such experiences, I am drawn to writers such as Phyllis Tickle, who speaks of feeling the Presence on the other side of a thin wall. Frankly, such experiences strengthen whatever resolve I have to resist treating anything else as if it were God. Non-verifiable experience? You bet. Still, it's there—and I've got lots of company when one looks back over the centuries.

2. As for Baptists and religious freedom, you know your history. You're also right about the public perception of the Baptist brand. There's more, though, to the contemporary story. Most Baptist bodies in the United States and the world continue to support religious freedom. The Baptist Joint Committee actively monitors the state of religious liberty in the United States and takes various actions designed to protect and foster such liberty. In any case, I think a deep commitment to genuine religious liberty remains a vital counterpoint to religious prejudice and violence.

3. "Spiritual formation, I think, always requires that we die in some sense in order to live an authentic human life." You're right. Similar sentiments exist in a range of religions. I also think it relates directly to our topic and text. In the case of the story, the Israelites have to die to the gods of Egypt in order to live well with the God who brought them out of Egypt. It's a multifaceted death involving perceptions, patterns of dependence, habits of speech, and the like. As quickly becomes apparent, it's hard to keep idolatry in the grave!

Much of our spiritual formation involves discerning and putting away idols, and this nearly always feels as if we are dying. "I can't do that. I can't live without it." We honestly believe our life depends on the idol.

We're right in a sense. When we put down an idol, the life we lived in service to the idol dies. Dying hurts. Much to our surprise, though, we find we outlive the idol and can do quite well without it, better in fact. Racism, imperialism, and the like rank as some of the big-time idols we must die to in our era. Of equal importance are the more personal idols, little household gods as it were: greed, fear of the other, vengeance, and their kin. Each one must be put away in favor of following the light we're given by the living God.

Rami: So beautifully put, Mike. I am always intrigued by your spiritual experience of the presence of God. And I love the image of the household gods of greed, fear, vengeance, etc. Wonderful!

There is a Jewish ceremony one does when moving into a new house or apartment. In addition to inviting guests to celebrate the move and to put the mezuzah on the door signifying the house as a Jewish home, we also use bread, salt, and a broom. The bread and salt are a way of asking that God never leave this household bereft of the basic necessities of life; the broom deals with your household gods.

Each guest is invited to sweep out one of the household idols saying, "may this home never be visited with anger," or "may this home never be visited by violence," etc.

In my own life, I have found that the household gods are highly portable. I carry them with me in the back of mind, and I listen to their litany: "you can't live without us; you can't live without us!"

This reminds me of what I said earlier about reading the "you shall not" of the commandments as meaning, "you are capable of doing without" or "you can live without." God's commandments are a direct refutation of the litany of the household gods.

I find it helpful to do more than listen to God speaking from the past, however. I have to actively cultivate my capacity to experience the presence of God here and now. While this experience itself is a matter of grace and is therefore beyond the control of the egoic mind, I do think it is both possible and wise to exercise our capacity to have the experience. Prayer, chanting, and meditation are my chief spiritual exercises.

My meditation is silent, so I have nothing to say about that, while my chanting is a bit complex and not readily explained in print, but the prayer I practice most is easily explained. It is called *gerushin* and is the Jewish equivalent of St. Paul's notion of "ceaseless prayer."

Gerushin means "to separate," as in to separate oneself from the harmful voices of the idols worshiped by one's ego. The practice is the ceaseless repetition of a name of God. I repeat *HaRachaman*, the Compassionate One.

This name is meaningful to me for several reasons. First, it is the name used by Reb Nachman of Breslov, an eighteenth-century Hasidic rebbe (spiritual master) from whose teachings I learned the practice. Second, my

Hebrew name, Rami, is short for *Rachmiel*, which means the compassion of God. And third, the root of the Hebrew word *rachmanut*, compassion, is *rechem*, womb. When I repeat *HaRachaman* I find myself embraced by the *Shekhinah*, the feminine noun Jews use for the presence of God.

Mike: I had forgotten the bread/salt/broom custom! Such actions have a kind of power, I think. If nothing more, they name the idols. The ritual also fuses mind, will, and body, thereby reinforcing the intent. You'll have to forgive me if I make use of the ritual in worship and other settings in the future!

Our recent postings also remind me of the importance of spiritual exercises. We agree, of course, that the experience of God comes as and when it will. Spiritual exercises have their place, though, and you describe it beautifully: they "exercise our capacity to have the experience."

I wonder if a wide range of the food, dress, worship, etc. laws might best be understood in such a light? Perhaps they were given not so much for their own sake or as arbitrary tests to be passed, but instead as exercises to strengthen the capacity for the experience of the presence of God.

Third Commandment

You shall not take the Name of YHVH Your God in vain; for YHVH will not hold him guiltless that takes His Name in vain. (Exodus 20:7)

Rami: Taking God's name in vain means using the name of God to bolster a position I know to be false, such as "I swear to God, the moon is made of green cheese!" My initial response to the Third Commandment hasn't changed since the third grade: "You mean I can lie as long as I don't use God's Name? Cool." While I didn't and don't believe that this is what Torah is saying, I am nonetheless intrigued as to why the Torah doesn't prohibit lying altogether.

Following Huston Smith, I would suggest that Torah is not laying out a complete ethical system in the Ten Commandments, but rather prohibiting actions that would promote the devolution of civilization as a whole. As such, the commandments beginning with number three are related to the Seven Laws of Noah (to which I will return a bit later).

Of course, it would be best if we didn't lie to one another, but this is highly impractical. I lie all the time both to protect myself and to protect others, and because it is often easier to say a half-truth ("I'm fine") than to involve someone else in my angst and drama. Actually, I am lying right now: even if I tell myself I am lying to protect others, I am most likely lying to protect myself from having to deal with the suffering of others. I lie because it is easier, requires less attention, and gets you off my back so I can get on with what I want to do. While some of the lies I tell are benign (or so I insist), others, if discovered, would cause great pain. But none of my lies undermine the political foundation of society.

Yet if I were to swear falsely in a court of law, and cover my lie by claiming under oath that it was the truth, the whole truth, so help me God, then my lie subverts justice, and in so doing threatens to bring down civilization as a whole.

I have more to say about this, but let me pause and invite you to get a word in edgewise.

Mike: "You shall not misuse the name of the Lord your God, for the Lord will not hold anyone blameless who misuses his name" (Exodus 20:7, *NIV*).

Like you, I have childhood memories associated with the text. In my case, most adults assumed the commandment prohibited cursing ("cussing," as we might say in the South) that used the term "god." Some of the more strict among us argued that the prohibition extended to such expressions as "gosh dang it," "golly," or just about any expression of anger, amazement, or ill will that began with the letters "g" and "o."

Amazing, isn't it? Even as a child, I thought it unlikely that God had slipped such a trivial matter into something as important as the Ten Commandments.

What does it mean to "take the name of the Lord your God in vain," as the King James Version puts it? My personal paraphrase is, "You shall not tie God's name to ungodly things." To put it another way, do not claim God endorses that which is evil. The prohibition is coupled with a warning: God will not hold you blameless if you do so.

Observing the commandment is difficult. To do so requires that we nurture both our knowledge of the living God (whatever the limits of such knowledge may be) and our openness to his presence. Such knowledge and relationship engenders "holy caution": that is, a growing awareness of how seldom we dare say, "Thus says the Lord."

Yet by its very existence, the commandment acknowledges that we will face times when we must speak. The moment we do so, the commandment shifts from the private to the public sphere. In the American South, the story of many white preachers and their support first of slavery and then of segregation provides the prime cautionary tale. Similarly, the story of black and (a few) white preachers who challenged the system and offered an alternative vision of equality serves as a hope-filled contrast.

Rami: It is interesting how quickly I went to legal matters while you went to personal ones. I think that speaks volumes about our respective cultural conditioning. While certainly not devoid of the personal spiritual dimension—the book of Psalms makes that clear enough—biblical Judaism is far more concerned with civil law and social norms. Matters of communal justice far outweigh matters of personal piety in the Hebrew Bible, and this focus on law still impacts the way rabbis read the text some 3,000 years after its compilation.

There is, of course, a personal element to the Jewish understanding of the Third Commandment. Like many people today, it was customary for the ancient Hebrews to bolster an argument with reference to God: "If this isn't the truth, may the Lord strike me down where I stand." Such statements can easily be abused, and this may be why Jesus says, "Let what you say be simply 'Yes' or 'No'; anything more than this comes from evil" (Matt 5:37). Which is a good segue to your point about God not endorsing evil.

You are right, of course, to point to those people of faith who used their faith to legitimize slavery, but can we really say this was a misuse of that faith? There are dozens and dozens of references to slaves in the Bible, and while the Torah clearly stands against the abuse of slaves, it does not condemn slavery but endorses it as a part of everyday life.

Nor is slavery the only evil God endorses. Genocide is clearly God's intent with regard to the Amalekites: "Now go and attack Amalek, and utterly destroy all that they have; do not spare them, but kill both man and woman, child and infant, ox and sheep, camel and donkey" (1 Sam 15:3). And then there is the matter of the Flood, the murder of the first-born Egyptians, and the slaughter of tens of thousands of Israelites who challenged Moses' dictatorship in favor of proto-democracy, to name but a few of the more troubling aspects of God's morality. The Bible isn't exactly a guide to liberal democratic values.

We can, as the history of Judaism and Christianity shows, make the Bible say anything we want it to say. This is why I cannot rely on the Bible for moral guidance. The text is too inclusive of different authors, times, worldviews, and cultures to give us a clear read on morality. Everything comes down to interpretation, which, regardless of the origin of the text, makes the Bible an all-too-human tool.

I have to pick and choose which biblical teachings to follow and which to reject. I have to decide for myself what is good and what is evil both in the Bible and in life. And while I find great wisdom in Micah 6:8, "Do justly, love mercy, and walk humbly with your God," I know that my take on justice, mercy, and humility is my own and not that of the Bible itself.

So I agree with the Third Commandment: don't use God to strengthen your own opinion; and I agree with Jesus: don't use God at all.

Mike: Yes, both of us reflect our respective cultural conditioning. My own tradition tends to practice a highly personal form of Christianity. Personal piety, of course, has deep roots in the Christian tradition. My faith journey (note: personal language again!) has led me to expand my range to include social/community matters. I have not felt it necessary to drop the personal dimension. In fact, I find the personal fuels the global, rather than vice versa.

Clearly the example of slavery rang your bell. We've been over this ground in previous postings. The two of us operate from different postulates with regard to the nature of God and the Scriptures. I rather doubt we will change one another's minds. On the basis of my postulates (see earlier postings), I indeed can say that the promotion of slavery was a misuse of Scripture and of the name of God. Given your postulates, you cannot. Both of us seek a place on which to stand and evaluate the relative merit of a given piece of Scripture. We've simply found different places.

In my last posting, I indicated more might be said about possible personal applications of the commandment. Over the course of my pastoral ministry, I've encountered cases in which God's name was invoked to justify spousal abuse, self-abuse, turning away from the poor, unjust war, church cliques battling to the death over worship styles, and religious leaders destroying the reputations or careers of theological rivals.

Pastoral ministry often consists of exposing such misuse of God's name, so that we might begin to address its root cause(s). Helping others to confess that they have been misusing God's name is often a necessary first step toward leading them to grow into responsible, faithful adults. In short, the Third Commandment is now an important component of my pastoral care toolbox.

Rami: Yes, we come from different perspectives about religion as well as from different religions. And the former is probably the greater difference between us.

I see religion as inherently social and political, one of the ways humans construct and enforce communal identity. As such, religion is given to creating hierarchies of power, in-groups and out-groups, and enemies both human and demonic. Religion keeps us constantly at war with "the other" and even with ourselves. By keeping us perpetually at war and afraid, religion fosters dependency on its leaders and its gods, both of whom offer us security even as they manipulate us into insecurity. Fear, not love, is the central operating system of religion.

If I understand you correctly, what you call your personal faith journey I would call spirituality. Spirituality can operate outside religion and fear, and root itself in humility, compassion, and justice. Spirituality, at least as

I experience it, isn't about security but about living fearlessly, embracing insecurity with a loving heart.

While I draw from Judaism and you from Christianity, we are both creating our own vantage points from which to judge the rightness of things. By definition, our respective vantage points must be outside the thing we are evaluating. So we are, each in our own way, heretics.

I wonder if it is possible to stand outside all systems, to stand free and unconditioned. The best I can do is to be aware of my conditioning by cultivating what is often called "witness consciousness," the capacity to stand outside one's opinions and recognize them as opinions. Once I am aware of my conditioning, I am no longer so conditioned by it. When I am aware of my conditioning, I am also aware of what I call the *te* of God: the way of forgiveness, truth, compassion, justice, etc.

I like what you say about the Third Commandment and your pastoral toolbox. We use God to excuse the cravings of ego, and in so doing mistake ego for God. Ego becomes the god we worship, and thus we violate both the Second and Third Commandments. Your congregation is lucky to have a pastor who can point this out in a manner that frees them from such idolatry, though I imagine they are not quick to praise you for it.

Mike: I'm not certain I buy into the hard and fast line you seem to draw between religion and spirituality. Life is more complicated, I think. Spirituality often functions as a kind of "voice of conscience" within institutional religion, challenging the "us versus them" way of thought and action, discerning the kinship of all humans, and reminding us that God cannot be confined within our structures.

Spirituality may well lead us to embrace life without the usual securities. It also may lead us back from forty days in the wilderness to speak a word of challenge to our religious structures even as we continue to attend religious services. Genuine spirituality ultimately requires us to love the neighbor, even the ones within our religious worlds. At its best, spirituality enables us to see a little farther and deeper than our home religious culture. We may then challenge the tradition, hoping to nudge it in the direction of a healthier vision of God.

To put it another way, we function as neighbors who have gone ahead of the group, around the bend or over the hill, so to speak. We return to say, "Come and see what I found." We cannot control the response of our neighbors. They may listen politely yet stay put. Some may label us heretics and take up stones against us. A few may go and see for themselves. Generally speaking, I think it requires at least a long human lifetime for a significant percentage of any religious people to respond positively. Sometimes, it seems to require centuries.

I wonder if we despair, at times, because the pace of response is so slow in relation to the brevity of our lives.

The Third Commandment strikes me as a word from the God we meet beyond the normal boundaries. Perhaps it's a word directed not only to those who rather casually claim God's endorsement but also, and most especially, to those who travel ahead. If so, the message might be phrased, "Remain thankful you've been allowed to peep around the next bend in the road; take care not to claim you've seen more than you've seen."

Rami: I agree that there is more to religion and spirituality than I have stated so far, and I like the idea that spirituality is, among other things, the conscience of religion. But then I would ask, where does this conscience come from?

It can't come from religion itself, for then it couldn't act as a corrective. It must come from outside religion. We might say it comes from God, but, unless we define God (which leaves us only with god), this affirmation says nothing. Yet I cannot deny my experience (and that of many others). When I find myself aware of the presence of God (the source and substance of all reality), I feel myself completely integrated with the whole of life and overwhelmed by a sense of love for and from all things. It is from this non-dual perspective that I understand St. Paul's teaching, "there is neither Jew nor Greek, there is neither slave nor free, there is no male and female, for you are all one in Christ Jesus" (Gal 3:28).

It is also important to note that spirituality isn't passive or quiescent. The spiritually infused person is a prophet who speaks truth to power and is willing to follow conscience all the way to the cross. When Jesus says, "take up your cross and follow me," he isn't inviting people to the Rapture, but to the crucifixion. He is saying (and demonstrating) that spiritual awakening engages one in the hard and dangerous work of pursuing justice. Justice and spirituality are two sides of the same coin of God-realization.

I am intrigued by your notion that it could take centuries for religions to turn the bend toward greater unity, justice, and compassion that is the hallmark of post-tribal globalism. I don't disagree, and this brings me back to my position that religion is a social device concerned with power more than truth, fear more than compassion, and control more than justice.

Religion doesn't necessarily lead people in a new direction. Most of the time, it simply creates a god who sanctions the direction in which the people are already moving. This is why true prophets are always a threat to the religious. Jesus, to mention just one example, often saw past Jewish tribalism and pointed toward a global spirituality, but Christianity (and I realize this is a gross oversimplification) ended up reinforcing that tribalism under another name.

As for despair, I admit to it. Conventional institutional religion as we know it, i.e., Bronze and Iron Age worldviews with their attendant biases, phobias, and mores, cannot move human consciousness to the more inclusive level of experience needed in the twenty-first century. But while I despair of religion, I do not despair of prophets. I place my hope in those contemporary spiritual pioneers in every religion who have "turned the bend" and left behind much of the madness that passes for faith today. These post-tribal prophets speak to humanity as a whole, and for the Earth herself. They sift through the old and find and release the timeless truths buried there. They may be Christians, Jews, Muslims, Hindus, or Buddhists by birth, training, and even affiliation, but they are not limited by these labels and are in fact practitioners of the perennial wisdom that flows through all faiths and is bound to none.

I prefer to see myself as a Jewish practitioner of this perennial wisdom, and I would dare suggest that you are a Christian practitioner of the same.

Mike: Our discussion in and around the Third Commandment brings the following to mind.

1. From my perspective, a sociological approach to "religion" has limited benefits. Yes, it helps us understand some of the roles (positive and negative) played by religion, but it cannot penetrate the inner heart of religion. Spirituality, personal journey, experience of the presence of God, calling, and a host of other terms or phrases attempt to describe the matter. All, of course, fall short. This "heart" lies within religion (theological structures, institutional frameworks, the individual, etc.). At any time, it may insist on being heard, whether through a single voice or a movement. So I think the "conscience" of religion resides within it, however deeply hidden it may seem at times. In Christian terms, I'm talking about the presence and work of the Holy Spirit, interfacing with the new kind of life God grants the individual.

All of the above is tied to the conviction that God is at work to save, reclaim, restore (pick your terms) not only individuals but also the whole of creation. Since this work takes place in history, it is inherently messy.

2. Would you argue seriously that modern Christianity or Reform Judaism (to pick two examples) is characterized by a Bronze or Iron Age worldview? I think it more accurate to say the Scriptures of both took shape in those eras. Both religious traditions, though, continue to rework their understanding and application of the Scriptures. In short, they are living religions that combine Scripture with experience, reason, internal and external conversations, and (let's hope) the Spirit of God to develop and modify their moral, social, and political positions.

3. All of which leads me back to the Third Commandment. Taken seriously, the commandment becomes a lodestone, leading a person of faith to practice serious self-restraint when it comes to speaking in the name of God. Practicing such self-restraint, in turn, helps us learn to distinguish our personal or culturally conditioned perspectives from whatever God's might be. Over time, we may even learn to say to ourselves, "Well, now. If I can't claim God endorses my position, just where did it come from?" Such a question may drive us to seek and confront the mundane, but powerful, sources of our narrowness. We may even feel compelled to abandon positions we've held and go in search of better ones. All this is part of spiritual formation.

Viewed in this manner, the Third Commandment's reach extends far beyond the courtroom. It penetrates into the deepest recesses of personal and institutional religion.

Rami: I would certainly agree that any one perspective on religion, be it sociological or otherwise, has its limitations. When I teach comparative religion at Middle Tennessee State University, I tend to focus more on the heart, the perennial wisdom that each religion shares, though I have to be careful not to impose my own bias on the religions we discuss.

I am so glad you brought the Holy Spirit, which we Jews call *Ruach HaKodesh*, into this conversation. *Ruach HaKodesh* is radically free, unconditioned, surprising. It is the way God works through the institutions of society; it is the way God raises up prophets who battle the powers that be to keep our institutions open and evolving. It is the way God breaks through the ego to liberate the soul. *Ruach HaKodesh* is divine poetry bringing ecstasy and meaning to the all-too-human prose of religious doctrine and creed. I worry, though, that organized religion tries to tame *Ruach HaKodesh* just as it tries to control God and align the Divine with the biases of the ruling elites. But as long as the Holy Spirit is capable of demolishing our egoic structures (both personal and communal) salvation, living a life surrendered to God and godliness, is possible.

As to Bronze and Iron Age worldviews penetrating modern expressions of Judaism and Christianity, I think it's a mixed bag. I can't speak for Christianity, but even modern Jewish prayer books speak of God in ways that are highly reminiscent of ancient times. We use metaphors such as King and Lord that are meaningless if not anathema to liberal, democratic Americans. We continue to speak of God as if God resided somewhere "out there" in time and space. Nowhere are the insights of modern cosmology included in our prayers. While most Jews live in 2008, we continue to pray as if it were 1008.

So, yes, Judaism is a living religion, but I often feel it is on life support. A true healing would require a radical openness to *Ruach HaKodesh*, empowering Jews to rewrite our prayers and refashion our theology so that they speak to what we know to be true and give meaning to life in the twenty-first century.

As for the practice of theological self-restraint, all I can say is, "Amen to that!"

Mike: We seem to have stumbled onto potentially common ground with regard to the Holy Spirit or Spirit of God, at least in terms of how the Spirit interfaces with personal and corporate religion. I'll look forward to seeing how this affects our unfolding discussion.

Language appears to be one of your underlying concerns. Certainly the use of terms such as "King" and the others you mention may foster inappropriate understandings of God. I sometimes long for updated language myself.

Yet—and there is almost always a "yet"—the language may serve a purpose the authors could not have envisioned. Having to deal with the language may force us to think seriously about modern assumptions. What's good and not so good about modern forms of democracy, individualism, and the like? Perhaps one could even say, if God is Lord or King, no one else has the right to claim ultimate authority over the world, others, or me. This kind of thinking may foster passive resistance to dictators, consumerism, or other would-be lords.

Fourth Commandment

Remember the Sabbath, to keep it holy. Six days you shall labor, and do all your work; but the seventh day is a Sabbath unto YHVH Your God, in it you shall not do any manner of work, you, nor your son, nor your daughter, nor your man-servant, nor your maid-servant, nor your cattle, nor the stranger that is within your gates; for in six days YHVH made heaven and earth, the sea, and all that in them is, and rested on the seventh day. Wherefore YHVH blessed the Sabbath day, and made it holy. (Exodus 20:8-11)

Rami: The Fourth Commandment deals with *Shabbat,* the Sabbath, and appears in two forms in the Bible. The first is in our text from Exodus, while the second occurs in Deuteronomy where the Israelites are commanded to "keep" rather than to "remember" the Sabbath, and offers a different rationale for doing so: "You shall remember that you were a slave in the land of Egypt, and HaShem your God brought you out from there with a mighty hand and an outstretched arm; therefore HaShem your God commanded you to keep the Sabbath day" (Deut 5:16). I take these changes very seriously.

The logic of the Exodus version is clear: God rested on the seventh day of creation, so you rest on the seventh day of the week. The logic of the Deuteronomy version is apparent only if we assume it is speaking to a different time and situation, which I believe it is.

The shift to "keeping" the Sabbath, paired with the injunction to remember slavery, suggests that the Deuteronomy text comes at a time when the people were having trouble extending the rights of *Shabbat* to slaves. By linking Sabbath observance to the Jews' own slave experience, the text is trying to soften their hearts that they might allow their slaves to rest on *Shabbat.*

The fact that the Bible condones slavery in the first place is problematic, but there is nothing we can do about that. The Bible does the best it can to protect slaves from abuse, but it cannot abolish slavery itself because slavery was too central to human socioeconomic-political reality. As a human document, the Bible cannot demand what humans cannot imagine, and a world without slaves was at that time unimaginable.

But the Bible can imagine, and in fact legislate, a world without abuse of slaves and others who are powerless in society: widows, children, orphans, strangers, etc. This is no small thing. And, thousands of years later, we have yet to create a society in which such abuse is absent. I say this not to excuse the Bible for its acceptance of slavery but to remind us of how revolutionary even this flawed document can be.

There is so much more to say, but let me stop here and invite you to jump in.

Mike: Like you, I think the Fourth Commandment is packed with meaning, some obvious, some less so. I find the commandment speaks to the following matters: time, rhythm, permission, community, and idolatry.

Time—the commandment sanctifies time, setting aside one day as a way of driving home that all time belongs to God.

Rhythm—the created live best when they set the rhythm of their lives by the divine rhythm.

Permission—God grants us permission to rest, in opposition to many cultures (including our own) that tend to devalue rest.

Community—as you suggest, the commandment casts ripples, thus challenging the ancient and modern tendency to dehumanize others.

Idolatry—offering the Sabbath to God calls us back from various idolatries (finding identity only in our work, treating work as the ultimate source of security, etc.).

Rami: Your mention of time made me think of Abraham Joshua Heschel, one of the great rabbis and sages of the twentieth century. Heschel called the Sabbath a "palace in time." It is an evocative term. When we think of palaces, we think of space, and when we think of space, we think of the things that define and fill that space. But time is something else.

Time isn't bounded by things or filled with things. Time is bounded by consciousness and filled with memory. Where a palace is all about tangibles, time is all about intangibles. So what are we to make of a "palace of time"?

I think Heschel is offering us a paradox that, if we can learn to hold it, has the potential to transform our lives. For one day each week, twenty-five hours in the traditional Jewish way of making the Sabbath, we are to live with the intangible. We are to live without having; we are simply to *be*. Having is the way the ego lives in the world: grasping and clinging to things and imagining itself as just one more thing. Being is the way the soul lives in the world: open, empty, engaged and engaging but not attached. The Sabbath is a day for soul living, for being rather than having. In this regard, I would say the best way to live the Sabbath is through play. Everything we do on the Sabbath should be done playfully, joyfully, and fearlessly.

Of course, learning to play the Sabbath may take practice, just like learning to play the violin or to play chess takes practice. But eventually you relax and just play. I think this idea of play works well with your ideas about rhythm, permission, community, and idolatry.

Too many of us imagine God's creation of the world as a very serious business. I imagine it is more like play. Play has its own rhythm, and a playful God would live attuned to that rhythm. Permission to play would be embedded in a creation that was the product of play, and play is so often communal, calling us to enhance the joy we derive from play by playing with others. Also, when we play, we smash the idols that enslave us. Idols only have power when taken seriously. Play is the enemy of the serious. True, play can become serious as it does in professional sports and the Olympics for example, but then it is no longer play. It is work.

Religion too often takes the play out of life and certainly out of the Sabbath, turning both into work. We are taught that we have to "earn" our living rather than to enjoy being alive. Imagine walking into synagogue on Saturday or church on Sunday and being invited to play: rather than singing well-worn hymns, we were given drums and cymbals and helped to create our own "joyful noise" (Ps 100:1). Rather than repeating fixed prayers we would, as Pentecostals and Korean Methodists do, open ourselves to the Spirit and pour out spontaneous hymns of praise. I'm not saying that there is no place for tradition, but there should also be room for play.

Mike: Many thanks for introducing the idea of "play"! I agree it provides one way to gather up rhythm, permission, community, and idolatry.

Play and formation go together. Think back to childhood. In my own case, many of my private games centered on various roles I might assume when I "grew up." Some were typical of my culture: farmer, truck driver, law officer, and the like. Others were atypical: public speaker, writer, and astronomer.

Such formative play required me to step outside time, at least time as I normally experienced it. While playing, I lived in an intense present moment. Past, future, and present more or less became one. I now think the experience provided a taste of eternity.

In addition, I felt free simply to try. Fear of failure and shame, overt concern about long-term results, fixation on who might be watching, what they might think, and other similar matters fell away. The fun, something I might even label "joy," sprang from my total engagement.

Sabbath offers something like this to all of us. Jesus once said, "Unless you become as one of these children, you shall not see the kingdom of God." Sabbath may be a way to relearn what most adults have forgotten—the practice of play in the presence of God.

Rami: You played "public speaker"? How did that work? Did you line up your stuffed animals and toy soldiers and then deliver speeches to them? I won't pursue this, but it is a bit weird. So let's get back to the Fourth Commandment: "remember" the Sabbath.

Are we simply called to remember that God rested on the seventh day? If this were the case, there would be no need to command us not to labor. Why should God's rest cause me to rest as well? Remember here means to imitate, to do as God did. Just as God worked for six days and rested on the seventh, so should we work for six days and rest on the seventh. But this begs the question, what did God do on the seventh day? The Torah doesn't tell us, so we are invited to guess. My guess is that God marveled on the seventh day; God sat back and looked at all God had done and just slipped into a state of wonder. If I'm right, then the Shabbat is a day for contemplating creation and marveling at the sheer wonder of it. And this contemplative marveling furthers God's call to liberation.

Let me explain: Torah tells us that the nature of reality is *tohu v'vohu*: wild, unformed, and chaotic (Gen 1:2). God doesn't defeat chaos, but lays creation over it as a kind of linguistic veneer: God speaks the world into existence. When we remember the Sabbath, we remember that we too use words to create order amid chaos, but we also remember how easily we may become so enamored of those words that we mistake them for reality. We make idols out of our words and worship them. I see this when people tell me Muslims don't pray to God but to Allah, refusing to accept the fact that Allah is simply Arabic for "God."

On the Sabbath, we marvel at creation and in so doing we remember the power and limitation of words. We remember how words can bring a sense of order to chaos, and how words can reify and become idols that distract us from the reality behind our words. When we rest on Shabbat we are invited to surrender our idols: our notions of surety, order, certainty, and security; and we are challenged to live one day without them; to live one day in the unknown and unknowable which is the presence of God.

Six days a week I do all I can to make sense out of life: to deny chaos or force it to conform to my understanding of order. This is exhausting. But on the seventh day I can give this up. I can let things be as they are: *tohu v'vohu*, wild and unconditioned.

We Jews speak of *Oneg Shabbat*, Sabbath joy, because when we allow reality to be reality, and realize we are not able to control it, we suddenly discover that we are able to navigate it. Remembering *Shabbat* teaches us how to surf the chaos rather than conquer it, and that insight just might make our living in the week to come much lighter and more loving.

Mike: In my own defense, I had best explain myself regarding playing "public speaker." Growing up on a farm, I often wandered for hours alongside the creek that flowed through our property. At some point, I began fashioning speeches (as well as short stories, but that's another tale for another day). I would develop, deliver, and rework each speech as I walked. Looking back, I now know I was doing the work of a writer and speaker: casting a first draft, revising it, trying on the revision, revising again, and the like. In the process, I found a kind of renewal, something I needed rather badly during my childhood years in an alcoholic home environment. We might even say the time spent alone functioned as a kind of Sabbath for me.

Now, back to the Fourth Commandment! Your comments on chaos, ordering words, laying down "our notions of surety, order, certainty, and security," and living "one day in the unknown and unknowable that is the presence of God" strike me as true. I love the image of surfing chaos. Surfers know better than to try to control waves. Joy comes in riding the wave as it is.

Much of the time we need a community to help us practice Sabbath in this fashion. Face facts. Almost nothing in our culture or daily life encourages us to surf chaos. Instead, we're told we need to take charge and make the world be what we want it to be. In short, we're taught to try to be God, or at least a kind of god. The longer we follow such a path, the wearier we become. The task is impossible, and we are not made for it anyway. Sabbath recalls us to our senses, reminds us of who and what we are, and encourages us to rest in God. It helps to be surrounded by others who share the experience.

However, let's not underestimate the potential of a private Sabbath. Go back to my boyhood days. My childhood environment, left unchallenged, would have shaped me in unhealthy ways. The time I spent alone, wandering by the creek, provided rest, time to think rather than do, and opportunity to remember who and what I was (as opposed to what the environment tried to impose on me). When I walked back from the creek and into my "daily life," I returned better able to surf its chaos.

Rami: Okay, so you weren't as weird as I had hoped. No problem.

You took my "surfing chaos" idea further than I did. You are absolutely right: the very notion that we are to take charge and forge our own destiny is a clear example of the ego playing God.

I also agree with you about "private Sabbaths." While the norm is to make the Sabbath a communal event, I prefer a day devoted to solitude and contemplative inquiry, allowing my mind to play freely without the strictures of fixed form and theological norms. My prayer life, in contrast to the official Jewish liturgy, contains a minimum of words. We talk too much during prayer, probably to avoid having to listen, question, or think.

And I couldn't agree more that our culture makes no time for chaos surfing. That is what the Sabbath is for, which is why we are to make it holy.

The Hebrew word for "holy" is *kadosh,* "to set aside." The Sabbath is a day set aside from the workweek in which we may "keep" (that is, participate in) the *te,* surfing along with What Is rather than concerning ourselves with What Should Be.

Why is this liberating? Because we are addicted to work, and that addiction is poisonous. We work not only to sustain ourselves physically but also to earn the means to satisfy a never-ending list of desires. We become obsessed with work because we are obsessed with having more and more stuff. This is why the rabbis, when they clarified the kinds of work prohibited on the Sabbath (*Mishnah Shabbat* 7), focused on the thirty-nine kinds of work associated with the building of the Tabernacle (sowing, plowing, reaping, weaving, spinning, erecting a building or demolishing one, and writing, to name just a few), all of which, if done for secular reasons, would result in increasing one's material wealth as well as one's desire for material wealth. Material wealth is so central to human thinking that, as both Calvinism and the Prosperity Gospel inadvertently reveal, we mistake the achievement of wealth for a sign of God's love. Shabbat is an antidote to this addictive spiritual materialism.

This is why the Jewish Sabbath liturgy eliminates all petitionary prayer. On the Sabbath, we don't ask God to change anything; instead, we practice loving what is. At the heart of this practice is not interfering with the natural flow of things and acting in a manner the Chinese Taoists call *wei wu wei*, non-coercive action. Acting with *wei wu wei* means living in accordance with *te* (the way of God, reality), i.e., cutting with the grain, swimming with the current, tacking with the wind, etc. Shabbat is the day on which we practice *wei wu wei*, or what I previously called surfing the chaos.

Mike: Your last posting prompts me to consider liberation and alignment.

The Sabbath, from my perspective, is a God-given opportunity to lay aside our "normal" preoccupations and assumptions and immerse ourselves in a radically different approach. Your point with regard to work, expanding desires, and non-coercive action is well taken.

The Sabbath is not an end in itself. Instead, it functions to form us into persons more nearly able to live in accord with God's way. Ideally, Sabbath extends its reach in our lives, so that the Sabbath perspective ultimately becomes our only perspective.

I suspect such full-scale transformation is not possible in the course of a human lifetime. Still, any number of persons may experience it to a significant degree, and they tend to catch our attention. Mother Teresa may be the best-known modern example within the Christian tradition.

I wonder how the Sabbath perspective might inform or transform congregational life, if allowed to do so. Any ideas?

Rami: Let me start with your notion that the Sabbath is an "opportunity to lay aside our normal preoccupations and assumptions and immerse ourselves in a radically different approach." Who would I be if I laid aside my normal preoccupations and assumptions? I can only think of one answer: I don't know.

I am my preoccupations and assumptions. I am the thoughts I think and the things I do, and I tend to think the same thoughts and do the same things day after day. My thoughts and my actions are largely conditioned by past thoughts and actions. So to ask who I would be without these is to ask a question I cannot answer, for the "me" that would answer it is the very "me" that would be put aside.

And yet this is exactly what is necessary if God's promise to "create a new heaven and a new earth [where] the former things shall not be remembered or come into mind" (Isa 65:17) is to be realized. The new is created when the old is forgotten and no longer comes to mind to be repeated.

Living without the former things, without conditioned thoughts and actions, means living without the learned biases that catalyze the fear, anger, greed, and violence that define so much of human existence. I wouldn't forget my name, but I would forget my labels. I wouldn't forget how to feed, clothe, or house myself, but I would forget why it is okay that others go hungry, naked, and homeless. I wouldn't forget the call for justice and compassion, but I would forget the excuses that allow for injustice and cruelty.

Jesus, rather than Mother Teresa, would be my role model here. Jesus challenged almost all the assumptions of his time. His table was open to all, something that is still unheard of. He dropped all labels and knew that "I and the Father are one" (John 10:30), an idea so terrifying that we imagine he meant that he and he alone was one with God.

Mother Teresa, on the other hand, as filled with compassion as she was, did not question assumptions and did not confront the system that made for the injustices she dealt with daily. To cite only one example: in a country like India, whose problems are so deeply rooted in overpopulation, she could not challenge the assumptions of her church and teach birth control.

As to your question of what a community steeped in Sabbath consciousness, and thus free from preoccupations and assumptions, would look like, I suspect it would look a lot like the early Jesus movement among the Jews. It would be a loose-knit community of people living lightly and lovingly, and seeing to the healing (on all levels) of everyone it encountered.

How do we transform our communities in this way? With twenty-five years of community leadership experience under my ever-expanding belt, I can honestly say I have no idea. I think that is one reason I left congregational life. It may be that the things needed to sustain a community are the very things that preclude the communal life I am suggesting.

It may be that what we are talking about can happen only among free individuals who gather for a moment to share a meal, a piece of wisdom, or a journey from one place to another without setting up any organization at all.

Mike: I want to play with another image. We might speak of Sabbath as a kind of cleansing, which washes away our self-centeredness and excuses, leaving behind only that which accords with the way of God. Perhaps it's not going too far to say that Sabbath continues the work often associated with baptism. Through Sabbath, we die to self and the world and are born anew.

The practice of Sabbath, then, serves as a means by which we become the kind of people who actually remember the God who brought us out of the narrow places, and who do not abuse the name (character, power, etc.) of God. Sabbath, in this sense, is a transforming spiritual discipline. The Sabbath truly is made for the sake of humanity, and not humanity for the sake of the Sabbath.

Can a community be or become a Sabbath community, or is the best we can hope is that individuals may become Sabbath persons who join loosely together in limited ways? You point to the early Jewish followers of Jesus as a possible example of this kind of community. I think you are right in describing them as people who, for the most part, traveled light. On the other hand, they also seem to have worshiped together daily, received or given ongoing instruction, and provided food to their needy. This sounds like a tightly knit community.

How did they achieve (at least on occasion) this balance between the individual and the community? They gave a great deal of credit to the Spirit of God. Would it be too much to say that a Sabbath community cannot be fashioned except God's Spirit take up the task? We look first to God, rather than techniques. Observing the Sabbath conditions us to accept this as so.

New heaven, new earth, new persons, and new community—Sabbath not only helps keep this vision alive but also proves to be a conduit through which the Spirit of God moves us toward its realization.

Rami: Yes, I would say Shabbat is, or could become, a day of spiritual cleansing. Seriously observant Jews actually prepare for the Sabbath on Friday afternoons by going to the *mikvah*, or ritual bath. The details of the *mikvah* are not relevant here, but suffice it to say this is a powerful act of physical cleansing and spiritual renewal. If we were to promote the Sabbath as a spiritual cleansing of sorts, I suggest we promote going to the *mikvah* to begin the spiritual cleansing with a physical cleansing as well.

If, as I believe, God is the Source and Substance of all reality, then God's body is the universe itself and everything in it, from quarks to quasars. My body is part of the Divine Body and should be honored as such. To think we can only get to the spirit by negating the body is to insist on a dichotomy that God would not recognize. Ritually washing the body is washing away not only physical dirt but everything that buries the truth of the body as a manifestation of God. This means washing away the illusions and delusions that pass for spiritual knowledge and wisdom; it means washing away the grim business of religion that we might rediscover the play of God.

I agree as well that the process of freeing ourselves from the false is, as you have said, a kind of death. Again, I am reminded of what the Sufis call "dying before you die." It is a psychological death; we die to the false and are reborn into the true, returning to God: the power that liberates us from the narrow places, the false idols, ideas, and conditionings, of our egos' creation.

As to your thought that this transformation, this death, cannot be affected by the ego itself, I would again happily agree. The ego cannot surrender itself to God, for the very thing that needs to be surrendered is the thing doing the surrendering. The ego must be surrendered by something greater than it, i.e., *Ruach HaKodesh*, the Holy Spirit.

So much of contemporary spirituality is simply the subtle machinations of the ego. The ego pretends to surrender as a means of maintaining control. True surrender happens only when the ego is pushed to the limit. This is what Twelve Step people call Hitting Rock Bottom, and what others might call the Dark Night of the Soul. Whatever we call it, it is only when the ego realizes it cannot save itself that it is surrendered to a Higher Power that can bring about salvation.

Sabbath Keepers might form communities, just as Twelve Steppers have their meetings, so I am not opposed to organization per se. I just worry that the organization will eventually take precedence over the practice and the message, at which point the whole thing is doomed.

Mike: Sabbath keeping, like everything else theological, becomes real to us only when we start to try to do it. It's a little like learning higher mathematics.

I remember how well I understood the teacher's explanation in class, only to find I understood nothing when alone in my dorm room with a particular problem. Comprehension and appreciation came slowly as I gradually solved the equation. I changed while engaging in the task, becoming less an observer of mathematicians at work and more nearly a mathematician.

We become mathematicians by doing math. We become Sabbath keepers by keeping Sabbath.

How might we get started?

For many of us, setting aside the time to participate in community worship might be the best way to start. Your earlier point is well taken. Community worship is too noisy, filled with words and actions. It usually is short on silence. Still, it breaks the typical rhythm of life. Worship's odd vocabulary, readings from ancient texts, hymns of varied quality, prayers and the like at least cut us loose from what we do most of the time. Perhaps the only way to begin to break our addiction to "the noise of life" is to substitute a different kind of "noise."

Beyond community worship, being still and silent before God helps. Some of us may be able to do this for an entire day. I suspect most of us need to start with something less ambitious. I find it useful to carve out some Sabbath time each day. If possible, I find a place where I can be alone. I sit with my eyes closed and my hands resting comfortably on my legs. If someone were to see me, he or she might think I was napping. I slow my breathing and wait quietly before God. This daily (well, almost daily) mini-Sabbath helps ground me in God.

You probably have additional suggestions. Certainly, numerous books and articles have been published in recent years on this subject. My fear is that many of us are daunted, afraid to try because we know we do not know how to do Sabbath. Getting started is the main thing.

Rami: I agree, Mike, that the only way to really get what the Sabbath is all about is to actually keep the Sabbath.

When Moses compiled the Book of the Covenant and read it to the Jews, they responded, saying, "*Naaseh v'nishmah*: We will do and we will understand" (Exod 24:7). The implication is that you cannot understand the deeper meaning of these teachings until you put them into practice. The doing reveals the meaning.

Unfortunately, most people no longer think this way. We want to understand why we should do something before we do it. This is like someone who has never tasted chocolate saying to a person who is offering her a taste of chocolate, "I won't taste it until you tell me what it tastes like." No matter how detailed the description, the only way to truly understand the nuances and magic of chocolate is to taste it for oneself. Hence the saying, "Taste and see that God is good" (Ps 34:8).

On the other hand, practice alone may not suffice. For example, without critique and guidance from a good writer, a poor writer will not learn to become a better writer simply by writing. Contra William Blake, a poor writer who persists in writing poorly will not become a better writer, let alone a good one.

To keep the Sabbath as a time for deep rest, play, and spiritual realization will require both doing and guidance.

Mike: By way of closing my portion of the discussion on Sabbath, I agree that we need guidance in order to better practice Sabbath. I'm a little more optimistic than you with regard to community worship.

Both our traditions provide for weekly community worship. Never mind that much of community worship as practiced simply strengthens our preoccupation with self. At its best, such worship ought to reignite our sense of the sacred.

Call me a populist, but community worship should attempt to offer this opportunity to the widest range of persons.

Fifth Commandment

Honor your father and your mother, that your days may be long upon the land which YHVH God gives you. (Exodus 20:12)

Rami: The Fifth Commandment seems simple enough. However, it raises two questions that merit investigation: what does it mean to "honor" our parents, and why will this result in our enduring in the Promised Land?

Let me address the first question here and see where our conversation goes.

While the commandment itself doesn't define what "honor" means, we can get some sense of the matter from other Torah passages. For example, children are forbidden to strike or curse their parents, and those that do so are to be put to death (Exod 21:15, 17; Lev 20:9); children are also forbidden to mock their fathers or disobey their mothers (Prov 30:17). The rabbis latter added a host of other rulings regarding honoring parents: children must provide needy parents with food, drink, clothing, shelter, and take them to and from their homes when they are infirm (Kiddushin 31b).

While all these behaviors are meritorious, the one thing one might expect to find is blatantly missing: nowhere are children commanded to love their parents.

I have heard it said that it is impossible to command love because love is an emotion and emotions are outside one's control. You can command behavior but not feelings, and that is why the Bible focuses on behavior. This makes sense when taken out of context, but since the Bible does command love—love of God, neighbor, stranger, and enemy—it clearly isn't afraid of commanding emotions. So why not do so in the case of parents?

I have also heard that love for one's parents is so natural that a command to that effect would be superfluous. But we know too much about human behavior to find this compelling. And, if doing what comes naturally makes commandments unnecessary, why outlaw sex with one's mother, since very few people are inclined to do that in the first place?

Another common argument is that the Fifth Commandment corrects the tendency to value love over care. People did naturally love their parents, but that love didn't necessarily translate into honor and respect, so the Bible made sure to command these explicitly.

I find none of these arguments convincing. For me, the meaning of the Fifth Commandment is this: it is easier to love strangers than intimates. It is easier to ignore or excuse the faults of people you rarely see while obsessing on the faults of those whom you see regularly. The closer you are to people, the harder it is to love them. So don't worry about loving your parents; simply make sure you take care of them.

This is harsh, but it may also be true. I can see how people can hold a grudge against one or both parents and use that grudge to excuse ill treatment and dishonor. "What did my dad ever do for me that I should go out of my way to see that he is taken care of?" "My mother abused or ignored me as a kid, so why should I bother with her welfare now that she is old?"

And the grudge doesn't even have to be real. The ego only cares for itself and will find any obligation to care for others, unless doing so somehow benefits the ego as well, to be annoying and meddlesome. So the ego will blow some minor childhood incident out of proportion to excuse indifference to the welfare of one's parents.

I have more to say about this, but let me catch my breath and give you a chance to jump in.

Mike: I've always been impressed by the Fifth Commandment's brevity. It says just enough to establish a behavioral standard, while remaining silent on less measurable matters, such as feelings. We're left to grapple with our feelings, even as we carry out the commandment.

Both of us know the familiar categories of love: brotherly love, erotic love, and God-like love (*agape*). The first requires that we grow to like each other. Eventually, "like" may develop into something deeper. Erotic love is biologically driven. *Agape* is a matter of the will, of deciding to want and to work toward the good of another. Feelings may well enter into the decision, but they are not a required prerequisite.

I divide the question of observance from the matter of feelings. For example, you write, "the Bible does command love . . . it clearly isn't afraid of commanding emotions." Insofar as I can tell, the Bible commands *agape*, which may be exercised with or without the emotion we call love.

The commandment, I think, is addressed primarily to adults, loosely defined. In my experience, adults are seldom able to change their feelings by an act of will. Repeated actions, though, may do so. To take an almost silly example, the best way to overcome our fear of water is to get in the water and learn to swim. After a few years, we may find our fear of water has dropped away. We may even transform into people who love the water. We do not achieve this transformation by paying too much attention to our feelings, but rather by paying careful attention—first to staying afloat and then to swimming.

We agree that the ego cares only for itself. I would add that it hates to have our attention diverted from it. Honoring one's father and mother may well divert our attention in this way. The ego fights back, of course. Spiritual formation is tough, dirty work—not least because it usually starts a civil war inside us.

Humble tasks train us to resist runaway ego. Providing food, drink, shelter, clothing, transportation, and the like is good for one's parents, but I suspect it's even more beneficial for us. It's the most commonly available "proving ground" for learning how to get out of ourselves and do what is necessary to build community.

Rami: I am struck by your insight into *agape* as a matter of will. As I understand it, *agape* is to be distinguished from *eros*, sexual love, and *philia*, non-sexual affection. *Agape* is divine in the sense that it is self-sacrificing. And therein lies my problem: how can anything willful be self-sacrificing? The very self that wills is the self that needs sacrificing. Can the self sacrifice itself? I don't think so. I think, as I have said earlier, that the self, the ego, cannot sacrifice itself and needs to be sacrificed by something greater than itself; call it the soul if you like.

I do agree, however, that feelings cannot be changed directly by the will. What I can change through will is my behavior, and what often happens when my behavior changes is that my feelings follow suit. But if I have to change my feelings before I alter my behavior, I suspect I will never alter my behavior. So this may be why the command to honor our parents is behaviorally defined by the rabbis: do the right thing by your parents and you may discover a deepening of love for them. But even if you don't, you have still honored them through your actions.

What we are talking about is a Zen Buddhist-based philosophy called Morita Therapy in Japan and Constructive Living here in the United States.

Shoma Morita was a contemporary of Sigmund Freud and chairperson of the Department of Psychiatry at Jikei University School of Medicine. My teacher David Reynolds, the founder of Constructive Living, was instrumental in "translating" Morita's insights for Americans. The key to Morita's teaching is the three-fold instruction: know your purpose; accept your feelings; and do what must be done.

Your purpose arises from discovering your rightful place in the universe. In Judeo-Christian terms, I would suggest our purpose is to "do justly, love mercy, and walk humbly" (Mic 6:8). At any given moment, our feelings may or may not jive with our purpose, but whether or not they align with justice, mercy, and humility, we are obligated to act in a manner that does.

Morita was primarily concerned with a type of anxiety or neurosis called *shinkeishitsu*, which we might translate loosely as "too much self-focus." As you said, the command to honor your parents is humbling and may well be part of the cure for *shinkeishitsu*, a problem from which all humans suffer.

We are basically in agreement, and I don't know if you have anything to add to this, but before we move on to the next commandment, what is your take on the connection between honoring our parents and living well on the land, which is the rationale the Torah itself offers for keeping the Fifth Commandment?

Mike: You wrote, "The very self that wills is the self that needs sacrificing. Can the self sacrifice itself? I don't think so . . . the self . . . needs to be sacrificed by something greater than itself; call it the soul if you like." Quite right! If one assumes we are on our own.

On the other hand, most Christians (including me) believe God sacrificed himself unto himself precisely in order to provide a way for each self to be made anew. God did what we cannot do and made it possible for us to participate in his kind of self-sacrificing life. So from my perspective, it is possible to grow toward *agape*, precisely because God has chosen to make it possible. It's certainly not easy. In fact, it usually hurts. Jesus' "Take up your cross and follow me" describes the experience.

My hunch is that our individual perspectives on God undergird what seems to be a genuine difference regarding our potential for self-sacrificing love.

On to your question: "What is your take on the connection between honoring our parents and living well on the land?" I think most standard translations read, "live long in the land." I start with the assumption that the commandment is part of a package of injunctions designed to form a particular kind of community. In this case, God's intent is that his people provide care for their aged parents. The commandment may apply to the individual son or daughter or to the community as a whole.

Assume the commandment was given while the Israelites were in the wilderness. If so, the temptation to discard elderly persons who could not keep up or who consumed valuable food and drink must have been quite real. The commandment might have had immediate application: "Let the community slow down, let all make do with less, that none—including the declining elderly—may go without what they need to live."

The temptation to discard the elderly did not go away once the community settled, though it may have taken other forms. In either case, the commandment assumes a stable community cannot be built and sustained if the weak are neglected or cast aside.

I tend to think the commandment has special relevance for modern society with its strong emphasis on production. What are we to do with people who can no longer produce more than they consume? At the least, our society, including the church for that matter, tends to want to hide them. However, the Fifth Commandment directly challenges our tendency to measure another's worth in terms of production. In fact, it suggests our worth is directly proportional to how well we care for the elderly (and, by extension, the weak in general).

Rami: Your reference to the cross reminds me of a panel I shared with Father Thomas Keating, one of my spiritual mentors. Someone asked him if the death and resurrection of Jesus Christ is absolutely necessary to salvation. Not wishing to be drawn into an argument about Christian exclusivism, Father Thomas gave a very diplomatic answer.

I then took the microphone and offered a different take: Yes, the death and resurrection of Jesus is absolutely necessary—necessary but not sufficient. Unless and until you are willing to die and be reborn, your salvation is not secured. Jesus is paradigmatic. He showed us what it is to live the kingdom of God, and what the consequences of doing so may be. Jesus says, "he who does not take up his cross and follow me is not worthy of me" (Matt 10:38).

In first-century Roman-occupied Jewish Palestine, the cross was a sign of state-sponsored terrorism. Tens of thousands of Jews and others were crucified by Rome as a warning not to challenge the power of Rome. To take up the cross meant to confront injustice, to stand up to the state and decry exploitation and oppression despite potentially fatal consequences. So Jesus is calling us to radical action. Yet there are several places in the Gospels where his radicalism seems to fly in the face the Fifth Commandment, and I would like to hear your take on these.

For example, in Luke 14:26, for example, Jesus says, "If anyone comes to me and does not hate his own father and mother and wife and children and brothers and sisters, yes, and even his own life, he cannot be my disciple." Similarly in Luke 9:60 Jesus says to a potential disciple who wished to bury his deceased father before joining Jesus, "Let the dead bury the dead." These sayings would be, and in fact still are, shocking to Jewish ears.

For Jews, hating family and hating one's life are considered a rejection of God (the One who gives life). And burying the dead is a cherished mitzvah (divine command). While it is true that Job said it would have been better had he not been born (Job 3:3), he was speaking out of pain. Jesus, on the other hand, seems to be making a general philosophical statement.

So rather than my guessing, and before we return to the notion of the land, what is your understanding of these teachings?

Mike: Whatever else might be said about them, our conversations are seldom predictable. Just when we think we're ready to move on to another topic, one of us pushes the other's hot button, and we strike off in an unexpected direction. I'll try to respond to the matters you raised.

1. "Jesus is paradigmatic." I agree. I would add, though, that he is something more. He indeed shows us what it is to live under the rule of God. In some way beyond certain definition, he may also grant us his kind of life. The nature of this kind of life is captured in the cross and the resurrection. We lay down our lives that we may be raised to a different sort of life. Few of us exhibit the new life to the degree of those you mention. Yet we also are not the people we would have been had we not received this new life.

I think of a certain aged man I've known a long time. He is crabby, a bit miserly, and harbors more than a dollop of racism in his heart. Sometimes I look at him and think how little he resembles Jesus. But I've known him a long time, and I remember what he was like before he died to his old self and rose to the new life God gave him. He now has a conscience, for one thing. He aches over his sin. He gives money to help the poor, though he still struggles with his miserly tendencies. He has actually spoken to his friends at a local cafe, challenging their racist jokes. Something new is taking hold in him. He is changing.

Certainly, Jesus is the example to whom he looks, but something more than example is at work here. A new kind of life has been planted in him, and it's trying to grow and root out its predecessor.

2. Christian exclusivism, as often understood and practiced, springs from a misreading of Jesus (in my opinion). Jesus commanded his disciples, then and now, to bear witness, receive new disciples, and build his kind of community. Insofar as I can tell, he did not authorize his disciples to persecute or even annoy those who chose not to embrace Christianity. Jesus seems to have believed he had "other followers" of which his disciples were not aware. He eschewed coercion. In short, he envisioned a community given to self-sacrifice, worship, and good works. This is the nature of his radicalism. We Christians have often failed to catch, let alone actualize, his vision. The vision, though, remains.

3. Luke 14:26 and 9:60 continue to shock us, especially if understood to refer to the emotion of hatred or the literal practice of burying the dead. Insofar as I can determine, Jesus had something else in mind. I think these sayings track back to "you shall have no other gods before me." Put positively, these sayings should be read in light of "Seek first the kingdom of God, and all these things shall be added unto you." Even good things and great obligations may sometimes function as idols, especially when used to excuse us from submitting to the rule of God.

If you want a contemporary example, consider patriotism. Love of country is often a natural good. When love of country trumps submission to the rule of God, it becomes an idol.

Rami: Thanks for your take on these things. I appreciate your interpretations of Jesus' sayings, though I suspect we could go much more deeply into them if we chose.

As for the link between caring for parents and thriving in the Promised Land, I think the Bible is reflecting the consensus of many Near Eastern legal codes that link inheritance of one's parents' property and wealth to the quality of care one provides for one's parents in their last years. Children can only inherit their parents' land if they honor them and provide for their welfare. The Torah is simply affirming the legal precedent that inheritance is not a birthright, as one might assume from the story of Jacob and Esau, but comes with personal responsibilities.

For example, having spent five years helping to care for my mother-in-law, I am acutely aware of the challenges posed to middle-aged children by aged, ill, and dying parents. I look to the health of my parents and worry that my sister, who lives quite close to them, will be burdened with their care, while I, who live hundreds of miles away, will not. This is an issue raised by the commandment, though not answered by it.

In addition to the personal challenges it poses, the Fifth Commandment also poses a societal challenge. Our society is segregated by age. Older middle-aged people frequently retire to children-free communities and put their parents in facilities for the elderly that are often little more than holding tanks for the near dead. The horrors and abuses that occur at old age and nursing homes are in the news regularly.

We live in a society that worships youth and fears old age. This may change as the boomer generation enters its final decades, but I fear that the lack of respect for the wisdom of the elder will remain even when the boomers themselves are the elders.

Abraham, Sarah, and Moses were in their eighties when God called them to lead. The Bible has a respect for the aged that our society lacks.

My rabbi, Zalman Schachter-Shalomi, has created a program for the elderly called "From Aging to Saging" and has written a wonderful book on the topic with the same name. He speaks of harvesting one's wisdom, going over what one has learned in the seventy or eighty or ninety years of one's life, and making it available to people. He asks the elderly, "Are you saved?" What he means by this is not theological, but technological. Just as you must remember to save your work on a hard drive if it is to endure the shutdown of your central processing unit, so you have to save your life wisdom so that it will survive the shutdown of your body. When people die unsaved, their wisdom dies with them.

One way to save your wisdom is to write an ethical will. In Judaism people are urged to keep an ethical will, a diary or journal of their life and what they have learned from living it. This ethical will is bequeathed to their children and grandchildren along with any property they may own.

This may seem far removed from "honoring our parents," but I see it as a way of doing this. We honor our parents when we honor their wisdom, and we honor their wisdom when we urge them to save that wisdom in an ethical will to be passed on upon their deaths.

Mike: I love what you shared about an "Ethical Will." In practice, it should strengthen the link between generations and conserve wisdom for ongoing use. This is the kind of project I would consider introducing to our church members.

In fact, your rabbi's program leads me to imagine other ways a community of faith might help people start to practice the Fifth Commandment.

1. Build prayer for parents into the ongoing worship life of the church. Nothing penetrates mind and heart better than something engrained in weekly services. Prayer, from my perspective, also may better align us with the purposes of God.

2. Find those who are actively engaged in appropriate support of their parents. Encourage and help them to frame their stories. Share the stories with the community of faith through print media, the web, and (on occasion) public testimony. Such stories challenge and inspire the rest of us.

3. Create support structures for those who honor their parents. For example, providing care in one's home can become exhausting. Caregivers often experience social isolation. Small support groups might be useful. Perhaps a church or synagogue might train "sitters" who can relieve the primary caregivers from time to time.

4. Face up to the reality that many parents will not be honored by their children. They will need another family. Church and synagogue might step into the role, at least partially. Our own church keeps a minister on staff. Her primary assignment is to befriend older adults, walk alongside them in every way possible, and help them find their way. For example, she has spent a great deal of time with senior adults, assisting them as they try to decide among numerous and confusing medical plans. She functions as a dutiful daughter to them.

I think we may be approaching a time of opportunity as the first generation of baby boomers enters stage-one retirement. I envision recruiting retired teachers, lawyers, physicians, and such to become surrogate caregivers to those more aged. Even a few such persons per church or synagogue would make an enormous difference in the lives of many isolated elderly people.

Of course, those who serve as caregivers would no doubt develop relationships with those they care for. Conversations would follow. The "wisdom" of the elderly might well begin to flow across generational lines. We might even learn not to fear old age, or at least to fear it less.

Sixth Commandment

You shall not murder. (Exodus 20:13)

Rami: It may be prudent to begin our discussion of the Sixth Commandment with a note on its translation. Some translations replace "murder" with the more generic "kill"; however, this translation is too broad and, in fact, puts the Sixth Commandment in conflict with other divine commands.

For example, in Genesis, people are allowed to eat fruits and vegetables (Gen 1:29), and doing so implies killing them. After the Flood, God allows humans to eat animals, though not their blood (Gen 9:3), and that certainly results in their deaths. And God sanctions killing other human beings both in warfare (Deut 20:1-20) and for violating certain laws such as the Sabbath, adultery, and murder itself (Exod 21:12-14; Lev 24:17, 21; Lev 20:10; Deut 22:22-24).

From the Jewish point of view, murder is the unlawful and, especially when we come to the rabbis, premeditated taking of a human life. The Torah's antipathy to murder has to do with disrespecting the image of God: whoever sheds human blood, humans will shed his blood, for in the image of God He made humankind (Gen 9:6).

Jesus spoke out against murder (Matt 5:21-26; Mark 10:17-19), as did Paul (Rom 1:18, 29-32; 13:8-10; Gal 5:19-21), James (Jas 2:8-11; 4:1-3), Peter (1 Pet 4:15-16) and John (Rev 9:20-21; 21:7-8; 22:14-15). So there really isn't any controversy here.

The rabbis noted that prohibitions against murder existed long before the Torah was revealed to Moses on Mount Sinai, and that the earlier book of Genesis already prohibited murder (Gen 9:6), so why include this prohibition among the Ten Commandments?

The rabbis' answer was that the Torah is far subtler than earlier law codes and refers to behaviors that one might not associate with murder. For example, causing a person significant embarrassment, failing to provide travelers with food, water, and safety, causing someone to lose her livelihood, passing legal judgment without the proper training, and failing to apply your wisdom to a situation that needs it are all tantamount to murder, though none are punishable as a capital crime. I admit that some of these are quite a stretch, but that is what rabbis do—stretch the text to cover issues not directly germane to the text. They seem to have understood "murder" to refer to various ways in which people's live are taken from them.

Due to this extension of the definition of "murder," the rabbis found themselves troubled by the death penalty. While the Torah makes it clear that the punishment for murder is death, the rabbis seemed to feel that taking a human life, even a murderer's, puts one on slippery moral ground. The evidence for this is that the rabbis put so many qualifications on proving someone a murderer as to make conviction next to impossible.

For example, the rabbis require that two eyewitnesses be present during the commission of the crime, and that these witnesses interrupt the murder in order to explain to the murderer the forbidden nature of his crime as well as the nature of the punishment associated with it. Just to be safe, the rabbis further demand that the murderer must have then affirmed to the witnesses that he was aware that murder was a criminal act and understood the likely consequences should he commit it.

Finally, in the rare event that all of the above were actually to take place, the rabbis decree that a murderer can only be tried by a tribunal of twenty-three judges, and only in the Temple in Jerusalem. When the judges vote, a majority of at least two is necessary for conviction. If, however, all twenty-three judges find the defendant guilty, the rabbis must annul the judgment because, since it is nearly impossible to get two rabbis, let alone twenty-three, to agree on anything, the unanimous nature of the verdict proves in and of itself that the defendant was denied vigorous defense counsel.

Given all of this, it is not surprising that the rabbis declare that any court that executes more than one person in seven years is to be labeled a blood-thirsty court. Rabbi Eleazar ben Azariah dissented, saying that the number should be seventy rather than seven.

Mike: "You shall not murder," or as a number of translations have it, "You shall not kill." Rami, I would be interested to hear more about your understanding of the term translated "murder" or "kill." One translation is more restrictive than the other, as you note. I rather doubt the earliest adherents had plant or animal life in mind, but certainly some modern sensibilities require this matter to be raised.

I think we agree that the commandment prohibits premeditated murder. Insofar as I can determine, no "out clause" is in effect. Premeditated murder is unacceptable, regardless of provocation. Taking the life of another denies the image of God found in each of us. This is wrong in several ways. First, the act attempts to destroy a work of God. Second, murder denies our essential kinship. Third, it is a kind of theft, isn't it—the taking of a life that may be said to belong to God and to the person murdered, but certainly not to us.

Murder amounts to an attempt to take the place of God. In Christian terms, murder finds its origin in the root cause of all sins: our attempt to be God unto ourselves.

Jesus, of course, argued that harboring hatred or despising another was a kind of murder. At first blush, this sounds strange. How can we possibly hope to control our feelings? Actually, though, I think Jesus had something else in mind. He understood that deep-rooted feelings sooner or later find a way to express themselves in words and deeds. Murderous feelings lead to murderous actions, including some of those you list (demeaning others, for example). Can't ghettos (of all sorts), genocide, and the like be said to start with hatred and contempt?

Of course, if we opt to translate the passage as "You shall not kill," we open up a broader range of concerns. Even if we stick with murder, though, the commandment seems to imply something larger. Once you refrain from premeditated murder because of your regard for the image of God in another, you've opened the door to many questions. I think your account of the rabbis and their reluctance to execute even a convicted murderer illustrates the point.

We probably need to talk about the possibility of a consistent life-affirming ethic as well.

Rami: I am not sure I have more to say about "murder" versus "killing." I was just looking at the Hebrew. The Torah uses the word *retzach*, to murder, rather than the more generic *harog*, to kill. I think what the Torah has in mind is extreme cases of premeditated murder.

The Ten Commandments tend to deal with those acts that, if committed, would undermine the very foundation of civilization. It is one thing if people lie; it is another if they lie under oath. I may have to accept the fact that people can't always be trusted to tell the truth, but if I cannot rely on the justice of the courts, then society itself if threatened.

Similarly, it is one thing if people kill; it is another if they kill premeditatedly, if they murder. Our secular legal code makes the same distinction. We distinguish between first- and second-degree murder, manslaughter, crimes of passion, etc. None of these is positive, but one is more threatening to civil order than the others.

Since the Torah has an additional six hundred and three commandments to work with, these ten are not meant to be the only laws in society but to highlight the breakpoints where the very existence of civilization is threatened.

Your argument that murder is "an attempt to take the place of God" is central to the argument against capital punishment and euthanasia, and leads directly into the need to articulate a consistent life-affirming ethic.

One issue that we have not yet touched on, but that cannot be avoided, is (of course) abortion. There is a part of me that would rather not tackle the abortion issue, not because I have any doubts as to my position, but because it may take us too far afield. So let me be as succinct as possible.

Let's start with the issue of when personhood begins. Notice I want to talk about personhood rather than life. Life isn't the issue, personhood is. A zygote, the cell that results from the fertilization of a human egg by human sperm, is life, but is it a person?

The Babylonian Talmud, the rabbinic code of law, states "an embryo is considered to be mere water until the fortieth day" (Yevamot 69b). After that, it is more than water but not yet human. Rashi, a twelfth-century rabbi and one of the most authoritative voices in Judaism, argues that a fetus is not a person (*lav nefesh hu*, "it has no soul") and references the Talmud's position that a fetus is *ubar yerech imo*, "like the thigh of its mother," i.e., it is a part of her body and not a separate person in its own right. The baby becomes a person only when its head—or, in the case of a feet-first birth, most of its body—has exited the mother's body.

The Torah text used to back this up is Exodus 21:22, which speaks of a case where a man causes a woman to miscarry. The man is not charged with murder unless the woman herself dies. He simply pays a fine for the death of the unborn baby, thus indicating that the baby is not yet a person.

Further, Judaism actually mandates abortion when the life of the mother is in danger, except, of course, when the baby has mostly exited the mother's body. Up until that point, if the unborn threatens the life of the mother, it is called a *rodef*, a pursuer, and is thought to be like a murderer who pursues you to take your life. Killing a *rodef* to save the life of another (in this case the mother) is a moral act.

All rabbis would agree with this. The differences among us arise when we begin to expand what we mean by saving the mother's life. Can we include psychological wellness? What about economic health?

As it was explained to me, the issue in Christianity is one of the soul. A mother who has been baptized has the chance to go to heaven, but an unbaptized baby does not. This is a mute point in Judaism, as the unborn are not thought to be ensouled. For us, the issue is one of relationships. The mother may have a spouse, other children, and/or elderly parents, all of whom rely on her. Their needs outweigh the needs of the unborn; so if an abortion is necessary to save the life of the mother, it is lawful.

Let me stop here and get your take on all of this. And let's carry this through to other issues like capital punishment, assisted suicide, and euthanasia.

Mike: While I knew the general position rabbis took with regard to abortion, I did not know the interpretive history that undergirds it. Thank you. I am intrigued by the idea of a *rodef* (a would-be murderous pursuer). To me, this sounds like a concept that might arise naturally in a time when childbirth entailed substantial danger to the mother. I suppose a successful birth (both mother and child safe) occasioned quite a celebration, as the *rodef* transformed into a blessing.

You wrote, "As it was explained to me, the issue in Christianity is one of the soul. A mother who was baptized has the chance to go to heaven, but an unbaptized baby does not." Certainly, this may have been an issue to medieval Christians, and it may remain one for some Christians today. However, many Christians long ago adopted a belief that unborn or young children who die are protected by the grace of God and so go to heaven. For such Christians, baptism is not an issue.

In America, at least, many Christians either oppose abortion or have deep qualms about it because they regard human life to be the gift of God. To take a human life is to usurp the place of God, and so amounts to murder. Of course, they, too, debate when human life (or personhood) begins.

Like the rabbis, many Christians argue that abortion is permissible in order to save the life of the mother, though we differ on the issue of how broadly "saving the mother's life" may be construed. Others argue that abortion is also permissible in the case of rape or incest. Very few American Christians argue for an unrestrained practice of abortion, and a fair number oppose abortion for any reason. Nearly all Christians regard abortion as a tragedy, part of the sadness of being a fallen human in a fallen world.

Christians divide rather sharply over how to interact with society with regard to abortion. Some attempt to use the tools of politics to write their position into the law of the land. Others restrict the application of the church's teachings to members of the church. A good number believe the decision must be left to the individual, whether alone or in conversation with their most trusted loved ones.

The Sixth Commandment, interestingly enough, is a foundational text for all of the above approaches.

Changing focus, Christians divide over the issue of capital punishment. The Hebrew Scripture and the New Testament allow for the state-sanctioned execution of those who commit premeditated murder. That being said, I tend to side with the rabbis! The taking of a human life is a grave matter. We now know for a fact that a sizable number of innocent people have been condemned to death via our justice system. The abolition of capital punishment seems to me to be the only way to ensure we do not take an innocent life. It may also deliver us from the temptation to become the kind of people who confuse revenge with justice.

I'll leave suicide, assisted suicide, and euthanasia for another post.

Rami: Regarding suicide, Louis Jacobs, a leading scholar in this area and author of *Suicide in Jewish Tradition and Literature*, most Jewish scholars do not link suicide with the Ten Commandments at all.

The Hebrew Bible has only two references to suicide. The first is found in 1 Samuel 31:4, where a badly wounded King Saul begs his archers to kill him so that he may avoid being taken captive and tortured by the Philistines. The second is in 2 Samuel 17:23, where Ahithophel, seeing that his rebellion against King David is lost, "set his house in order, and hanged himself." Interestingly enough, the Bible does not condemn or even comment on either act, and suicide is not among the prohibitions articulated by early Jewish sages.

The Talmud, too, makes no mention of suicide, though it does tell the story of Rabbi Chanina ben Teradion who was burned alive by the Romans in the presence of his students. The latter urged him to breathe in the smoke in order to hasten his death, but he refused, saying, "It is better that God

Who gave me my soul should take it rather than I should cause injury to myself." It is only in a post-Talmudic rabbinic text called *Semachot* that we find a negative attitude toward suicide:

> He who destroys himself consciously, we do not engage ourselves with his funeral in any way. We do not tear the garments, and we do not bare the shoulder in mourning, and we do not say eulogies for him; but we do stand in the mourner's row and recite the blessing of the mourners because the latter is for the honor of the living. (Semachot, Chapter 2)

The key here is that to declare someone a suicide, we must know that he destroyed himself "consciously," i.e., intentionally. Because we can never truly know another's intentions, the rabbis go out of their way to find mitigating circumstances such as illness, acute stress, fear, or pain to declare the death not to be a suicide. They even argue that only a person who calmly and dispassionately announces he or she is going to commit suicide and then does so immediately can be counted as a true suicide.

With regard to euthanasia, Judaism rejects active euthanasia but not passive euthanasia. Jews do not have to prolong life against all odds; we can discontinue procedures that are preventing nature from taking its course; and doctors can administer dangerous, though not definitely lethal, amounts of painkillers like morphine even at the risk of causing cardiac arrest as long as the intent is to relieve pain and not to kill the patient. Once again, intent is the key, and because intent is nearly impossible to ascertain, Judaism can be strongly opposed to certain behaviors in theory and yet very open hearted and nonjudgmental toward those behaviors in practice.

This is all somewhat academic, so let me share a personal story. One of my students at MTSU came to me a few years ago distraught over the apparent suicide of a close friend of his. He worried about his friend's fate in heaven.

My student's dad, a Southern Baptist pastor, told him that regardless of how the boy lived, his suicide condemned him to the fires of hell for all eternity. My student was hoping I could provide an alternative view. I explained that the general rule in Judaism is that at the last minute, as he was dying, his friend regretted his action, and therefore the death would be ruled accidental rather than a suicide. Thus the boy's friend would go to heaven, not hell. This proved too lenient, and my student went back to the harsher ruling of his father. What is it about us that we require the suffering of others to justify our own heartlessness?

Mike: Insofar as I can determine, neither the Hebrew Bible nor the New Testament deals with suicide per se. During the Middle Ages, the Western Church (at least) developed a teaching regarding those who committed suicide. The theory argued that to take one's own life was to usurp God's rightful place. Suicide came to be regarded as a kind of rebellion against God that left no opportunity for repentance. The practice of denying burial on holy ground to suicides dates from this era as well.

In my experience, I find most Christians have not studied the matter. Instead, they've picked up on the medieval concept via movies, popular literature, and conversations with friends.

My personal perspective is that the medieval position is unbiblical. It caters to our desire to judge others, a desire Jesus warned us to resist: "Judge not."

When we separate theology from a pastoral connection with living and dying persons, heartless logic often replaces love as the lodestone of religion. It seems to me that God's love/grace is sufficient to cover the kinds of pain that may lead to suicide. The church's task, then, is to comfort the bereaved and commend the departed into God's hands.

Your story about the student connects with my own experience as a pastor and a human being. My response to your student would be the same response I give to others in such a circumstance: "Your loved one is in the hands of God, who is gracious. I suspect the two of you will meet again in the presence of God, where you will find your friend fully healed and filled with new life."

God's grace, rather than questions about human intentions, is the foundation on which my position rests. The practical result, though, is that the rabbis and I once again have found our way to common ground.

Like many Christians, I reject active euthanasia. To intentionally take a human life crosses a line I do not think the Bible allows us to cross. Passive euthanasia, on the other hand, may well be an act of faith. We may choose to trust God, accept that our life is coming to a natural end, and refuse medical procedures that may stretch our living days without providing an ounce more of good life. This amounts to saying, "Into your hands I commit my spirit."

Rami: Before we move on, let me respond to the issue of judging and to the larger question you raised earlier about articulating a "life-affirming" ethical position of our own.

I find Jesus' teaching to "judge not, and you will not be judged; condemn not, and you will not be condemned; forgive, and you will be forgiven" (Luke 6:37) very important. We have an innate desire to judge others, and Jesus challenges us to overcome it. I am not sure this is possible or even wise. But if we make a distinction between judging and being judgmental, then I think it is both.

I judge all the time, and right living requires that I do so. But I have to recognize that I often base my judgments on flimsy evidence and limited if not faulty data. So I have to be humble about the judgments I make, and I have to be willing to reconsider my judgments when the facts warrant it. In this I avoid becoming rigid in my thinking and judgmental in my personality.

This is where I would separate Jesus from the church, and almost every prophet from the institution that grows up around him or her. Institutions, by their nature, not only judge but condemn; and in doing so they pervert the teachings of their founders. This is why the Hebrew prophets are forever attacking the Jewish establishment, and why I find it so difficult to align myself with any religious institution.

Now, on to your point about articulating our own ethical stances.

I am always looking to identify some essential teaching from which to derive a viable global ethics. I suspect the Golden Rule is the most universal teaching humankind has ever articulated. To quote the rabbinic version, "Do not do unto others what you would not want others to do unto you" (Shabbat 31a). This, its author Rabbi Hillel said, is the whole of Torah.

Not one to argue with Hillel, I would nevertheless suggest that there is an assumption even more basic that provides the foundation for his ethic: "Let us create humankind in our image after our likeness" (Gen 1:26). Or, as the modern Jewish sage, mystic, and activist Abraham Joshua Heschel put it in his essay, "No Religion Is an Island," the human being is "a disclosure of the divine, and all men are one in God's care for man. Many things on earth are precious, some are holy, humanity is the holy of holies. . . . To meet a human being is an opportunity to sense the image of God, the presence of God." This mystical core energizes Heschel's and Hillel's ethics. Each and every person is sacred.

If I begin with this premise, the irreducible sacredness of every human person, I must be against all human exploitation, oppression, injustice, war, murder, torture, and capital punishment. But what about abortion and euthanasia?

Regarding abortion the question is not "when does human life begin?" but "when does human personhood begin?" I take "human life" every time I cut my hair, as each follicle contains my DNA. No, the issue isn't life but personhood, and the fact is we cannot say for certain when human personhood begins.

I am no more comfortable with assigning personhood to a zygote than I am withholding it from a baby until it has exited its mother's body. The answer lies somewhere in between, but precisely where, we don't know. And because we don't know, we ought to be conservative in our thinking.

On the face of it, I would argue that abortion after the first trimester (or certainly the second), except in the case of saving the life of the mother, is wrong. Prior to that, the decision should be left up to the mother, her physician, and anyone else she chooses to consult.

Euthanasia is more challenging. If I focus on personhood, what do I do with someone in a vegetative state? Personhood is gone, so is euthanasia permissible? I would say "yes." But do I have to be reduced to a vegetative state to be relieved of my suffering? What if I am dying and in terrible and unremitting pain? Can I not choose my own fate? Certainly I don't want the state to decide for me, but what about deciding for myself? Or, if that is no longer possible, letting those who love me and would only act in accordance with my desire decide?

Here I would argue that the sacredness of human life includes respect for the choices a person makes regarding her or his own death. I would accept euthanasia and suicide as just, compassionate, and even holy decisions in certain cases. Denying me the freedom to end my life with dignity when that life is irreversibly fated for a protracted, painful, and ignoble death would be an insult to the divine image that manifests as me.

These are just preliminary thoughts, and I am more than happy to reconsider all of it, though a detailed exploration of ethics will most likely take us far from our stated goal of dealing with the Ten Commandments.

Mike: I do not think I have much more to add at this point about euthanasia and abortion, unless we wish to take off on an extended excursus from the commandment itself. At the same time, I want to respond to a few of your points.

1. We agree on the meaning of "judge not, lest you be judged." Judgmentalism is what Jesus had in mind. The tendency is deeply embedded

both in individuals and institutions, though it may take on frightening proportions via the power of an institution.

2. I also agree that Jesus is separate from the church. Because this is so, he challenges the church's self-serving ways (even as he does for the individual). Each small and large reform movement in the church hopes it springs from a fresh apprehension of Jesus' intent. No reform lasts forever. In fact, most lose steam after one generation or less and lapse into institution building. Still, there is a corrective element outside the church, and when all is said and done Jesus is that element.

3. Strangely enough, Jesus is also within the church. He may be found in the Scriptures, in traditions, and in the work of the Spirit. In my experience, he sometimes appears in the face or voice of another, especially in "the least of these." Years ago I developed a self-discipline I try to practice when dealing with others. Silently throughout the encounter, I remind myself, "She (he), too, is a child of God, one made in the image of God. Act accordingly." I think this is similar to what you have in mind.

In any case, it works when I allow it to do so. My attitude and actions are changed, so that I become less self-centered and more able to pay attention to the person before me, hopefully in a way that proves helpful. The discipline provokes a kind of reformation in me. My hunch is that the church would become and remain more nearly the movement of Jesus' intention if its leaders and members embraced a similar discipline.

Rami: Before moving on to the Seventh Commandment, I want to briefly offer something to your personal practice of remembering that the people you meet are the Image and Likeness of God.

The Name of God, Y-H-V-H, when written vertically in Hebrew, looks like a stick figure drawing of a human being. It became a spiritual practice to visualize the Name of God as the physical body of any person you meet: the *Yod* is the head, the *Hey* is the shoulders and arms, the *Vav* is the torso, and the final *Hey* is the pelvis and legs:

The practice is to see oneself and everyone else as this Name, the Image and Likeness of God. With this visualization comes a desire to treat oneself and others as manifestations of God, which is to say that we treat all people—and I would say all beings—with utmost respect, compassion, and justice. When I lead retreats I often begin

with having the participants write the Name of God in this fashion and place it in their sleeping rooms as reminders that they and all they encounter are God's Image and Likeness.

Chapter 7

Seventh Commandment

You shall not commit adultery. (Exodus 20:13)

Rami: The Seventh Commandment seems straightforward enough, but nothing in Judaism is simple.

Technically, the Seventh Commandment refers to a man having sexual intercourse with a married woman, an act that carries with it a death sentence for both of them: "If any man commit adultery with the wife of another and defile his neighbor's wife, let them be put to death both the adulterer and the adulteress" (Lev 20:10; Deut 22:22).

While the Bible does not specify the means by which adulterers are put to death, the rabbis ruled it was to be death by strangulation. As with all capital crimes, in order to be convicted of adultery, two witnesses must interrupt you and explain to you the grave consequences of your behavior. If, after you and your partner both affirm that you understand the rules and the consequences for breaking them, you choose to persist in the crime, well . . . it's your hanging. Chances are, however, the moment has passed, and you go home to watch a ball game on television instead.

By the way, a married man having intercourse with an unmarried woman is not, according to the Torah, committing adultery. While his wife may wish to strangle him, the court does not. Obviously we are dealing with a society in which women were the property of their men, and the real crime here is for a wife to have sex with a man other than her husband.

Because some believe Judaism is all about actions rather than thoughts, it is sometimes said that Jesus expands the idea of adultery in a very unJewish way: "everyone who looks at a woman lustfully has already committed adultery with her in his heart" (Matt 5:28). However, the ancient rabbis made a similar argument, saying that a man who gazes lustfully upon a married woman is also an adulterer (Leviticus Rabbah 23:12). Jesus simply expands the field to *all* women, not just married ones.

When dealing with adultery, the book of Numbers (5:12-31) introduces one of the oddest practices in biblical Judaism: *sotah* ("goes astray"). When a man suspects his wife of adultery, she is given a choice. She can accept a divorce or drink "bitter waters" into which the Name of God has been dissolved. If she opts for the latter and is guilty of adultery, the water will kill her instantly. If she is innocent of the charge, she will live.

Notice that it is up to the woman how to handle her situation. She is not required to admit her guilt or prove her innocence. In fact, her innocence is, in a sense, presumed, as the first words of the priest to the woman are, "If no man has lain with you, if you have not gone astray in defilement while married to your husband, be immune to harm from this water of bitterness . . ." (Num 5:19). The woman can simply say, "You know what? I don't want to be married to a jerk who accuses me of cheating on him. I'll take the divorce." Or she can drink the bitter waters and prove her innocence, in which case she is then stuck with her suspicion-prone mate.

Chances are the origins of *sotah* go back to the Code of Hammurabi, which states that a woman whose husband accuses her of adultery should, on her own volition and to protect the self-esteem of her husband, throw herself into a river. If she survives, she is innocent. If she drowns, she is guilty. Hammurabi and Numbers together probably motivated the good Puritans of Salem to take women accused of witchcraft, weigh them down with chains, and toss them into the river to see if they float. If they do, they are witches. If they don't, they are not. Of course, they are dead, but that seems to be a price men are willing to pay.

My people were not totally blind to the injustice of focusing only on women, however. According to the rabbis of the Talmud (*Sotah* 27b), the bitter waters work on both parties involved in an adulterous relationship. Although it is the woman who is under suspicion, and it is she who must drink the water, the magic works on her lover as well. If she is guilty, he dies instantly right along with her. But, if she is innocent, she is rewarded for her loyalty by becoming pregnant even if she is barren.

To illustrate this point, the rabbis say that Chana, wife of the prophet Samuel, was barren and prayed constantly for God to give her a child. When God seemed to ignore her and she remained childless, the rabbis say she threatened God, telling Him that she would make Samuel suspicious that she was having an adulterous affair, drink the bitter waters, and, because she was innocent, thereby force God to give her a child (*Brachot* 31b). God, like most men, gave in, and Chana got her baby.

Nachmanides, an early medieval rabbinic sage (1194–1270), points out that of all the commandments in the Torah, only this one requires the active intervention and participation of God. The water kills only by an act of divine intervention. There is no poison in the drink, only the Name of God. If the woman is guilty, God intervenes and kills both her and her lover. And if she is innocent, she lives, and He gives her a baby. It is also interesting that *sotah* is the only commandment requiring the desecration of God's Name, a fact that argues for the importance of marital fidelity in Judaism.

The question I can't help ask of this practice is this: How many people died because of it? While many Jews find the practice sexist, I wonder if in fact it is the opposite. Since there is no poison in the potion, and since I doubt that God really engages with humans this way, any deaths resulting from *sotah* would be psychosomatic. I'm not condoning the practice, but I can't help but imagine it let almost everyone off the hook.

I am sure you didn't expect all this, and that you will masterfully get us back on track, but this is what rabbis do, and I felt compelled to do it.

Mike: Far from being overwhelmed, I rather enjoyed the guided tour. My guess is that the death penalty, which came to be attached to the commandment, drove the developments you outlined. Once again, the rabbis appear to have sought ways to reduce the chance that the penalty might actually be applied. If so, I stand with them.

When I reflect on the Seventh Commandment, several things come to mind.

First, it was and is intended to protect community. Trust of any kind between adults is impossible if one must always be on watch to make sure nobody "steals" one's spouse!

Second, the commandment challenges our biology. For better or worse, we appear to be a species that values monogamy yet finds its consistent practice very difficult. Chalk it up to our fallenness or to evolution—either way, many humans have a wandering eye. Thus Jesus ups the stakes considerably when he insists that lust is equivalent to adultery.

We may react in at least two ways. A fair percentage of us ignore the commandment as unrealistic. The argument goes something like this: we have a biological drive to have multiple sexual partners over the course of a lifetime; therefore, we have little choice but to do so. In fact, "the rules" (whether the commandment or some other stricture) ought to give way to our need.

At the opposite extreme are those who seek to honor the commandment by denying the essential goodness of the human sexual drive. Their line of reasoning might be described as follows: God has forbidden satisfying the sexual impulse with anyone other than our marriage partner; therefore, the impulse itself must be a sin; sex must be restricted to procreation and the sexual impulse guarded against at all other times.

Neither approach takes God, community, or the human condition seriously. Healthy boundaries are necessary if one is to manage one's humanity, take part in developing community, or learn to live in harmony with God and enjoy his gifts appropriately. The Seventh Commandment is one such boundary condition.

Third, by implication, the commandment places quite a burden on married persons. If a marriage is to be immunized against adultery, both partners must work at building a relationship deep and satisfying enough to bind themselves to one another. Listening, courtesy, kindness, giving one another room while never losing touch, shared tasks, clearing hurdles together, the worship of God, and the like build such a bond, given time.

Fourth, Christians have long associated fidelity in marriage with fidelity to God. Blame it on Hosea, if you will. The Christian point is that marriage (along with parenthood) provides an excellent, comprehensible way to begin to fathom the dynamics of the God/human relationship.

Finally, the commandment implies strongly that we cannot easily separate individual morality (for lack of a better term) from matters of the family and the larger community.

Rami: Your point that the Seventh Commandment is designed to protect community is well taken. As I think I said quite a while ago, I suspect, following Huston Smith, that all ten of the Ten Commandments point to those acts that, if committed, would lead to a breakdown of society.

I agree regarding monogamy as well. While we uphold the ideal of lifelong monogamy, as a society we practice serial monogamy, or more accurately serial marriage. We marry for a while, then divorce, and then marry again. This provides us with legal cover for the biological imperative to have multiple partners.

You mention two ways people deal with this commandment: they either ignore it in favor of multiple partners or take it to mean that we ought to damn sex itself. There is a third alternative, God's alternative, you might say, if you take the Bible as the literal word of God, and that is polygamy. Taking multiple wives, and being bound to them legally, economically, morally, etc., is the way God handles the problem. Still sexist, of course, but God is hardly a feminist. Nowhere does the Hebrew Bible condemn polygamy. On the contrary, it regulates it.

Exodus 21:10 says, "If a man takes another wife he shall not diminish the food, clothing, or marital rights of the first wife." Deuteronomy 21:15-17 says that the firstborn son of a polygamist family has the right of inheritance even if his father favors another wife and her children and despises his mother. And Deuteronomy 17:17 warns kings against taking too many wives.

And then there is the practice of Levirate marriage where the brother of a man who dies childless is obligated to marry his sister-in-law, even if he himself is already married, and have children with her, assuming the sister-in-law agrees (Deut 25:5-10).

Of course, we can argue that there were valid socioeconomic and cultural reasons for all of this, but that doesn't negate the fact that the Bible does not ban polygamy. In fact, polygamy wasn't banned in Judaism until the *Herem* (ban) of Rabbenu Gershom in the eleventh century, and that only applied to Ashkenazi or European Jews. Sephardi and Mizrachi Jews (Jews from Portugal, Spain, Arab countries, and Iran) never banned polygamy, though most dropped the practice as they immigrated to countries that outlawed it. Modern Israel limits the practice but makes room for polygamous families emigrating from countries where polygamy is legal.

My point is that this practice has a long history of legality. In the United States, polygamy is in the news a lot lately, and people are officially offended by it. But the real offense, it seems to me, is child marriage and rape. That these are happening under the cover of polygamy is a crime, but consenting adults who wish to practice plural marriage . . . they may be on to something.

I want to come back to the holiness of sex later, but let me stop here and invite your comments.

Mike: One of the things I enjoy about our conversation is how your mind pivots to point in unexpected directions. Polygamy was not on my radar!

Your summary of the relevant history is on target. I did not know the particulars of medieval Jewish regulations, but I am familiar with the Hebrew Bible's approach to the subject. "Regulation" captures it nicely. For the most part, the biblical regulations seem to have been designed to protect the woman or women involved. Perhaps the same was true of the medieval legislation, or was it developed primarily to reduce the chance of legal or mob persecution?

Getting back to the Bible, I have to wonder how many men in ancient Israel could afford polygamy. Was monogamy more nearly the norm? Either way, the commandment against adultery would apply, thus restricting men's conduct more than was normal in the ancient world.

As I've noted in earlier entries, I think God starts where we are and tries to move us as far as possible toward his ideal. His work is formation work. As a result, I need not agree with the premise that "God favors polygamy." In fact, I think the practice belongs to an earlier era. I do believe, though, that God favors fidelity in marriage, both for the kinds of practical reasons either of us might list and because it's good training for a man or woman who would become faithful to God.

Both of us, I think, sometimes engage in a bit of hyperbole. For example, you write that our society practices serial monogamy. I would argue that a percentage of our society does so. Observation leads me to add, though, that some individuals seem never to practice monogamy of any kind. Remarkably, some portion of the population does. Monogamy, therefore, is possible, though individuals may (and do) find it very difficult for any number of reasons.

If monogamy is so hard, and in some ways runs counter to our biology, why would God require it? We've already alluded to the benefits to society and the possible benefits to women, at least in ancient times. I suggest the deeper reasons are that it is good for us in general and good for our relationship with God.

Growing in the ability to give another person exclusive devotion strengthens character, develops charity, and encourages a growing acknowledgment of one's own rough spots and foibles. All such developments are good for us.

Furthermore, such developments may lead us to better comprehend and accept the faithfulness of God and the challenge we present to that faithfulness. That's good for us, too. We come to see that, far from our being "a great catch," we are in fact quite flawed, and the wonder is that God pursues and stays with us at all!

Rami: Hyperbole? Hyperbole! This is outrageous, sir, and I demand . . . . Yes, in fact, I love hyperbole. But, this terrible slander aside, I agree that the

Bible at its best, which in all honesty means the Bible as I choose to understand it, is moving us into alignment with the *te* (way) of God: doing justly, loving compassion, and walking humbly.

There are a few other issues I would like to raise here before we move on to the next commandment. The first is the story of Jesus and the adulterous woman presented in the Gospel According to John. The second is the role of celibacy in early Christianity and the Catholic Church. And the third is the possibility of articulating a sacred sexuality based on the Song of Songs. The latter two may seem far-fetched, but I think this commandment opens the door.

Let's discuss each separately, beginning with the story in John. Here is the passage:

> Early in the morning he came again to the temple. All the people came to him and he sat down and began to teach them. The scribes and the Pharisees brought a woman who had been caught in adultery; and making her stand before all of them, they said to him, "Teacher, this woman was caught in the very act of committing adultery. Now in the law Moses commanded us to stone such women. Now what do you say?" They said this to test him, so that they might have some charge to bring against him. Jesus bent down and wrote with his finger on the ground. When they kept on questioning him, he straightened up and said to them, "Let anyone among you who is without sin be the first to throw a stone at her." And once again he bent down and wrote on the ground. When they heard it, they went away, one by one, beginning with the elders; and Jesus was left alone with the woman standing before him. Jesus straightened up and said to her, "Woman, where are they? Has no one condemned you?" She said, "No one, sir." And Jesus said, "Neither do I condemn you. Go your way, and from now on do not sin again." (John 8:2-11)

First, let me say I love this story: with this one text Jesus puts an end to the obsession with condemnation that marks so much religion in his time and ours. Second, let me admit that it poses problems for me as well. Chief among these is the fact that, by the time of Jesus, the law regarding adultery and capital punishment had already been changed from the biblical form mentioned in John. The Sadducees might have followed the older law, but not the Pharisees.

John tells us that the woman had been "caught" in the act of adultery. The story hinges on the fact that adultery is a capital offense, and we went into the details of convicting people of such offenses in our discussion of the commandment against murder. So, with those legal requirements in mind, let's assume that the two witnesses who caught her followed the rabbinic law of Jesus' day and interrupted the adulterous couple to explain to them that, if they continued in their lovemaking, they would be executed. And let's imagine further that the lovers stopped, listened to what the witnesses had to say, verbally affirmed they knew what they were doing and what would happen to them after they did it, and then, in full view of the witnesses (how else could they witness the act?), the couple returned to their now public lovemaking. Even if all of this took place, there is still a problem: where is the woman's lover? According to the law, both of them must be executed. And, my final point, the means of execution in Jesus' time was strangulation, not stoning. So what gives?

Bart Ehrman, in *Misquoting Jesus*, notes that this story does not appear in the earliest manuscripts of John and may have been a later addition inserted by copyists who were not up on rabbinic jurisprudence in the time of Jesus. I suspect something along these lines is the case. The story is written in such a way as to highlight Jesus' differences with the Pharisees and to underscore the triumph of compassion over law.

Regardless of how the text got into the Gospel, if you take it as gospel, what do you make of it, and how do you handle the fact (a fact at least to me) that the church seems to have sided with the faux-Pharisees of John rather than John's Jesus?

We desperately need Jesus in our time: a prophet of God who can force the country and the world to look at the evil it does while hiding behind the mask of law, and who can affirm the triumph of justice and compassion over legally mandated corruption and oppression. Yet the people who are the most Jesus-obsessed seem to align themselves with the stone-throwers. With no malice intended, and with only a deep sorrow in my heart, as one who loves Jesus and the Judaism he taught, I must admit that Christianity, or more accurately the Christianity of many conservative evangelicals and fundamentalists, disappoints and frightens me terribly.

On to another aspect of this story. I am totally intrigued by the two mentions of Jesus writing something on the ground. Jesus wrote on the ground in response to the Pharisees' challenge, "Now what do you say?" And he returns to his writing after saying, "Let anyone among you who is without sin be the first to throw a stone." No one bothers to read what Jesus wrote, and John doesn't bother to tell us what he wrote, yet this is the only time in the Bible that Jesus writes anything! If this were still a Jewish text subject to the *midrashic* mind that revels in this kind of puzzle, there would be dozens of stories focusing on what Jesus wrote. For Christians, the question may be mute, but as a Jew who sees Jesus as a Jew, I find it compelling.

What are your thoughts on this story and on the "missing writings of Jesus"? Actually, now that I think about it, a book purporting to reveal what Jesus wrote, and its relevance for our lives and salvation, would be bigger than the *Prayer of Jabez* and *The DaVinci Code* combined. How's that for hyperbole?

Mike: Okay. Let's follow your agenda, starting with John 8:1-11.

Who doesn't love the story? It appeals to us in a number of ways: the shift from condemnation to empathy-driven response; the confounding of wrong-headed religious authority by its challenger, Jesus; the drama of the story itself; and the phrase that has become part of our culture ("Let he who is without sin cast the first stone").

To the best of my knowledge, all major modern commentaries assume the story was added to John's Gospel. Many skip it altogether, others deal with it in footnotes or appendices, but all admit it does not quite fit John. At the same time, the story had become embedded in John long before the New Testament canon was debated and finalized. It is part of the canon, and most Christians treat it as such. That is, we assume it "belongs" in John and has something vital to say to us.

Rami, in glancing through several sources, I find few commentators allude in any way to the penalty of strangulation. Instead, they refer to Deuteronomy and assume stoning remained the penalty. Some say the *Mishnah* also teaches this was so. On the other hand, Christian commentators nearly always note several issues. For example, the "scribes and Pharisees" present no witnesses, as required by Mosiac law. In addition, the presumably guilty man is strangely absent. Finally, the accusers' words seem to imply that only the woman was to be held accountable.

Obviously, such matters do not square well with first-century practice. I do not think the storyteller (or inserter) cared much about such things. What is the story's point? Let's unpack the tale and see.

A crowd, led by "scribes and Pharisees," drags a woman "caught in adultery" before Jesus for judgment. As the story makes clear, they don't particularly care about the woman or the case at hand. Their goal is to entrap Jesus, to force him to make a choice between their brand of religious authority-driven justice and some alternative. If Jesus opts to condone their perspective and actions, any threat he presents is defused. On the other hand, if Jesus dares denounce their position, he can more easily be branded dangerous and portrayed as "the enemy." This is classic cutthroat politics, whether in the first or twenty-first century.

Jesus simply refuses to play the game. In the story, he bends down twice to write on the ground. Some modern commentators argue that these actions had well-understood implications in the first-century world, at least in the Middle East. Writing on the ground would have been recognized as his refusal to engage the matter verbally (as they wanted) or on their terms.

The religious leaders decline to accept his response and press for a verbal response. They want to hear a declaration of judgment: "Stone her," or "Free her." Jesus confounds them all. When he looks up and says, "Let him who is without sin cast the first stone," he changes the grounds of the dispute from "who is to blame and how shall we punish her" to "who among you, indeed, dares claim to be without sin and entitled to pass such judgment." Even the most respected among the scribes and Pharisees present cannot pass the test. Jesus then writes in the dirt again, signaling that he is finished with them. Recognizing either their own sin, or at least that this encounter is over, the crowd slowly departs.

Only the woman remains. To this point, no one has spoken a word to her. Her accusers treated her as an object, a tool in their hands to use against Jesus. Jesus speaks to her. Interestingly enough, he says nothing about her purported specific sin, about that which may or may not be part of her past. Instead, Jesus treats her as someone now freed from all accusation. He focuses on her potential future. In effect, he says, "You have the gift of a new start; make good use of it."

Now, as to your point about the church's tendency to side with the accusers, you're sadly correct. This may drive us to despair if we believe in a one-time cure for "our bent to sinning." I (and most Christians, I think) do not harbor such optimism. In fact, many of us argue that when we read such stories we ought to place ourselves within them, not with Jesus but most often among those opposed to Jesus. Only then might we really hear his words and be called back to our senses.

Even if we experience such a recall, we dare not assume we are "cured" of the human tendency to practice judgmentalism or use others to protect our own interests. We see the "cure" more nearly as a kind of lifelong, daily treatment. Some respond to the treatment better than others, but anyone may be made better than would otherwise have been the case.

Tracking back to the Seventh Commandment, we might say Jesus taught us to take it seriously in our own lives yet never to use it as a means to hurt another, heighten our own stature in the community, or protect our theological turf.

Rami: Let me quickly respond to the source issue regarding strangulation. According to David Daube in his 1973 book *The New Testament and Rabbinic Judaism* (p. 307), the Romans outlawed stoning by Jewish courts, fearing that stoning drew crowds, and crowds often turned into anti-Roman mobs. Because of this, the rabbis opted for strangulation, an act that could be performed more discretely. Seeing the creativity of the Jews in this regard, the Romans then outlawed capital punishment by Jewish courts altogether.

The Talmud goes into this at length, especially in tractate *Sanhedrin* (50a) where the rabbis argue that if a priest's daughter commits adultery the punishment needs to be more severe than strangulation and opt for burning instead. This, however, is more an example of rabbis with too much time on their hands since the same tractate says ten pages earlier (41a) that the Jewish courts no longer have the legal authority to execute anyone (the Romans reserved this for themselves), and so adultery could only be punished by whipping.

I am very interested in the idea that even knowing that a text was added to a Gospel (in this case the story of the adulterous woman in the Gospel According to John), it can still be accepted as being the word of God. This would, to my mind, invalidate the notion of biblical inerrancy. If you can't trust this text to be gospel, how can you trust any text? And if the answer is that it fits, meaning that the message is in line with the Jesus of faith, then the arbiter of what is and what isn't true is the reader rather than God. This makes us all part of the Jesus Seminar, voting our particular bias, and pretending that doing so somehow tells us something about the text. I have no problem with this. In fact that is what I think we all do, albeit unconsciously, but for many Christians I know removing even one block of text threatens to topple the whole tower of Bible (I couldn't resist the pun).

What I am hearing in your comments is that by refusing to play the game of supporting or rejecting the status quo, Jesus is offering a third way when it comes to dealing with Judaism and the Jewish realities of his day. I believe that this third way is vitally needed today, and I look forward to exploring it with you.

I am also intrigued that Jesus never forgives the woman and only refuses to condemn her. He tells her to "go her way"—her way rather than his way—and "sin no more." I read this in light of Jewish teaching. First, rabbis cannot forgive other people, so there is nothing surprising about Jesus' action or lack thereof. Second, his focus on "sin no more" is the Jewish practice of *teshuvah*, literally "turning": as in "Turn from evil and do good" (Ps 34:11) and "Cease to do evil, learn to do good" (Isa 1:16-17). So here, again, I think Jesus speaks for and within the classical rabbinic tradition.

I like your interpretation of the story, Mike. I would say we are, each of us, the adulterous woman betraying God's love for us. If we die in sin, we die cut off from God. If we live, we have a chance to live differently, to turn and repair (what Jews call *tikkun*) our relationship with God.

As I mentioned earlier, our conversation about adultery has clearly broadened into a more general discussion of sexuality. With that in mind, I want to ask you about the concept of celibacy. Jesus says, "For there are eunuchs who have been so from birth, and there are eunuchs who have been made eunuchs by men, and there are eunuchs who have made themselves eunuchs for the sake of the kingdom of heaven. He who is able to receive this let him receive it" (Matt 19:12). I am one who cannot receive it.

A eunuch is a castrated male. The word comes from the Greek meaning "bedroom guards," so it is clear these men were castrated by the fathers or husbands of the women whose bedrooms they were guarding. Judaism, however, prohibits castration of both men and animals. Leviticus 21:20 even prohibits men with crushed or mutilated testicles from entering the assembly of the Lord, and Leviticus 22:24 prohibits castrating animals and the use of castrated animals in Temple sacrifice. So what are we to make of Jesus' celebration of castration?

I have been told that I am taking the text too literally, and Jesus is really referring to celibacy. But this, too, is troubling from a Jewish point of view. Every time God established a covenant in the Torah—with Adam (Gen 1:28), with Noah (Gen 9:1), with Jacob (Gen 35:10-12), and with Moses (Lev 26:9)—God called them to be "fruitful and multiply." From the Jewish point of view, celibacy violates God's plan.

There is, however, the exception of the apocalyptic Jewish sect of the Essenes. Philo, the Jewish philosopher, and Josephus, the Jewish historian, mention celibacy as an Essene practice. Philo writes, "[Essenes] repudiate marriage; and at the same time they practice continence in an eminent degree . . ." (*Hypothetica* 11:14).

And Josephus writes, "These Essenes reject pleasures as an evil, but esteem continence, and the conquest over our passions, to be virtue. They neglect wedlock. . . . They do not absolutely deny the fitness of marriage, and the succession of mankind thereby continued; but they guard against the lascivious behavior of women, and are persuaded that none of them preserve their fidelity to one man" (*Jewish War* 2.8.2).

The Essenes expected the End of Days was at hand, and for that reason they had no need to be fruitful and multiply. They also believed that women were by nature promiscuous, which would make it all the more difficult for men to abstain from sex if marriage were allowed. Do you think it was Jesus' apocalyptic tendencies that had him celebrate celibacy (while in no way denigrating women)?

Do you think this kind of thinking influenced the Apostle Paul when he wrote, "To the unmarried and the widows it is better to remain single as I do. But if they cannot exercise self-control, they should marry, for it is better to marry than to burn with passion" (1 Cor 7:8-9)?

And what of the Essene "rejecting pleasures as an evil"? Again the Essenes were in no sense mainstream. Judaism sees pleasure and sexual pleasure in particular as a gift of God. We are even taught that when we die we are brought before God not to explain the evils we have done but to explain why we rejected any of the legitimate pleasures that God offered us while alive (*Jerusalem Talmud*, Kiddushin 4:12), including sexual pleasure.

So, assuming Jesus said what Matthew says he said, this is one example of Jesus making a clear break with the normative Judaism of his day. Because Jesus' position is not normative in Judaism, the issue for us Jews is mute, but I don't understand celibacy, and I cannot help wonder what impact it has had and continues to have on Christianity (in all its forms). What does it do to a faith when for centuries its spiritual formation was in the hands of celibate and frequently misogynist men?

Mike: If possible, I want to respond to your questions via one entry. As I see it, you raise the following matters: the legal/political context of John 8:1-12, canonization, and celibacy.

1. Christian scholars are familiar with the way the Roman government reserved capital punishment for itself. With reference to the story in John 8:1-12, this reinforces the strange nature of the entire event. It was "out of order" in almost every way possible. To my mind, this strengthens the case

for the event being a planned political/religious test of Jesus, an attempt either to co-opt or discredit him.

2. "Biblical inerrancy" is a relatively modern concept, a by-product of the Enlightenment rather than a historic Christian affirmation. Interestingly enough, it developed in roughly the same period as the idea of papal infalli-bility. The ancient church, insofar as I can tell, took a different approach to the Scriptures. For the sake of brevity, I'll illustrate the ancient approach by outlining the canonization process.

Most, perhaps all, of the writings that would become the New Testament were produced during the first century in the decades following the ministry of Jesus. None of these documents were regarded as Scripture. Instead, they, and other documents as well, were circulated among the churches. As the years passed, some documents came to be read over and over again, to be found to have lasting value so to speak. Various church leaders began to compose lists of the writings that were used by the vast majority of the churches.

Eventually, the church leadership gathered and debated which of the writings ought to be regarded by all the churches as Scripture, that is, as works useful and holy in the same sense as the Hebrew Bible. Three criteria applied. Is the work the product of an apostle or someone closely associated with an apostle? Has the church universally found the work good for wor-ship and instruction? Does the work in some sense contain the gospel? To put it another way, they sought some historical connection to Jesus, took the church's experience seriously, and asked one key theological question. At the end of the process, the leadership made a decision to recognize what we now know as the New Testament: the "canon" of Christian Scripture.

For the most part, Christians regard the process as closed. The New Testament, regardless of how various parts originated or found their way into the text, is the church's book—good enough for the purpose for which it was given, namely to instruct us for "salvation" and all that may entail.

The canonization process, in some ways, mirrors the human/divine nature of all of Scripture. It certainly ought to remind us that the Bible is not God or a "fourth person in the Divine One." The Bible, instead, is a tool designed to draw us to God, draw us back when we wander, and draw us to one another in community. Given this perspective, the legitimacy of any given text in the canon is not called into question by lower or higher "criti-cism."

3. Celibacy is an apt topic within a wider discussion of sexuality. Very few Christians in any era have taken Matthew 19:12 literally. I certainly do not. At the same time, the words of Jesus forced the early church to break with normative Judaism and accept actual eunuchs, and others who were mutilated or injured or ill, as full-fledged members of the Christian family. As far as I can determine, such things did not exclude a person from membership or leadership in the ancient church. It's one of the few instances in which the ancient church ran ahead of its surrounding culture.

Protestants and the Orthodox tradition disagree with Roman Catholics over celibacy with regard to clergy. Yet all three traditions, I think, admit that celibacy may be a calling, a part of one's vocation. Celibacy has often been driven by a sort of dualism, i.e., the tendency to divide the world into flesh and spirit, and to see the flesh as evil and the spirit as good, but at its best it serves a better purpose: freeing one to devote one's energy solely to prayer, worship, study, and ministry to others.

As for misogyny, it's certainly been part of the scene. All human sins we might name have been as well! Sins affect, distort, and diminish the church. Yet I believe God works with such fragile and flawed vessels as individuals and groups and even institutions. For example, the well-known poet and Christian writer Kathleen Norris, without denying any of the negatives, has found that many monks believe and act as if women are "made in the image of God" and are therefore good. History provides many stories of celibates who learned to practice hospitality, friendship, and self-sacrificial service. In short, from a Christian perspective, I do not think celibacy is to be sought, but God may offer the gift. In that case, it should be accepted, as we would (hopefully) accept any other gift offered by God.

Rami: This was very interesting, Mike, and I learned a lot from it. I'm especially taken with your notion, which you have shared before, that "God works with such fragile and flawed vessels" as humans and our institutions.

Mainstream Judaism never imagined a "Fall" (we speak of the "expulsion from Eden" rather than the "Fall"), and for us the universe is, as Genesis says, *tov*: intrinsically holy and perfectible. Our experience of things, however, is broken. We imagine ourselves to be alien, sinful, cut off from God and creation. We then project this brokenness onto others and onto nature itself. While I think it is a psychological rather than ontological brokenness, working with brokenness and the shadow-side of humanity and our institutions (what Paul calls "the Powers" perhaps) is vital to a truly redemptive, healing, and transformative spirituality. And part of that healing involves a re-imagining of sexuality, so let's move on to that.

My *Rebbe,* (spiritual teacher) Rabbi Zalman Shachter-Shalomi, defines sacred sexuality as a recovery of our authentic physicality that is capable of experiencing a level of bliss that transcends mere pleasure. He calls it a form of communion that fills us with awe.

The first step toward reclaiming this authentic physicality is to recognize the universe as God's body. Creation is an extension of the Creator just as sunlight is an extension of the sun. Seeing the universe as God manifest in time and place, and discovering that our role in creation is to be that aspect of nature that knows life to be divine, is vital to sacred sexuality. Once this is understood, and so far it is only the mystic geniuses of our various religious traditions who seem to get it, every encounter is sacred. The touch, taste, sounds, etc. of lovers and life itself are all part of a sacred sexuality.

I'm not talking about genital sexuality exclusively. The genital reductionism that marks the pseudo-sexual revolution of secular society (say that five times fast) makes sacred sexuality impossible. I'm talking about a sexuality that Sigmund Freud called "polymorphously perverse," where your whole body and being is alive to the bliss of life. To paraphrase Reb Zalman: Love is as basic and as binding in the universe as gravity.

With the exception of *Shir HaShirim* (Song of Songs), the Torah's near obsession with sex has nothing to do with the sacred and everything to do with power, with men owning and controlling women. But this is genital politics and not sacred sexuality with its capacity to, as Reb Zalman says, transport us to a different level of existence where the world is drenched in a loving and overwhelming sense of at-oneness.

When the world is seen as God's Body, the ecstatic glimpse into greater levels of reality is possible through all kinds of sensual encounters: smelling a rose, feeling the bark of a tree, petting a cat, listening to the ocean lap the shore, eating a peanut butter sandwich, etc.

How does this connect to the Bible? I suggest we look to *Shir HaShirim,* the Song of Songs.

When the rabbis sought to fix the biblical canon, among the books they intended to leave out was the Song of Songs. Rabbi Akiva, perhaps the greatest sage of his day, argued that if the Hebrew Bible is holy, the Song of Songs is the "holy of holies." Indeed, he argued, the entire Way of God could be derived from the Song of Songs alone. Why? Because it is a celebration of love, sensuality, sexuality, and union with God through love of another.

The lovers in the Song are poetic expressions of that level of divine intimacy through this-worldly meeting that Martin Buber called "I and Thou." When someone is seen as *Thou*, he or she is seen as a manifestation of God. And the only way a person can see a *Thou* is if she looks through the eyes of an *I*, a Self-realized or God-realized human being. When *I* meets *Thou*, it is God meeting God.

Too often we Westerners, rejecting our Hebraic sensuality for Neo-Platonic asceticism, deny the most precious gift of God's love: His Body as the world. It seems to me that Christianity, as the religion of Incarnation, could be (I would even say should be) the vehicle for bringing the gift of the ecstatic communion with God's Body to humanity.

Christianity hasn't done this because it insists that only Jesus is the Incarnated God, where I would say that Jesus is paradigmatic of one who realizes that the universe itself is God incarnate.

Anyway, I'm rambling. I only mean to use the negative "You shall not commit adultery" as a pointer to the positive, a true sexual revolution rooted in *Shir HaShirim* and the communion of *I and Thou* as the key to living the kingdom of God on, in, and through the Body of God, life herself.

Mike: Before responding to your take on sexuality, I need to say a word about "Fall."

Christians typically think of the human condition as one of fallenness. We differ considerably over the degree of fallenness. The attitudes range from "the image of God within us is marred" to "humankind is totally depraved." Some Christians would agree with you that fallenness is psychological rather than ontological, though such distinctions get a bit fuzzy when dealing with something as complicated as a human being. Regardless of our differences, most of us think fallenness is a real element of human life, both for individuals and for the human community.

That being said, you and I agree about the necessity of "working with brokenness and the shadow-side of humanity and our institutions" being "vital to a truly redemptive, healing, and transformative spirituality." So on to sexuality!

While you recognize the universe as "God's body . . . an extension of the Creator just as sunlight is an extension of the sun," I see the universe as God's creation. For Christians like me, the universe in all its complexity, simplicity, and discreet parts is sacred in that it is God's work. To put it another way, creation is sacramental—through it God may touch us and we may touch God. This includes other individuals, so that "every encounter," indeed, is sacred.

Our capacity to love each other, to break through to deep and genuine intimacy, to feel at one with another, is a gift from God. Sexual love, like any sensual experience, may be a means to this end, and ideally it should always be so. When we experience "at-oneness" with another, we may at least sense that love is the unifying power of all God's creation.

Westerners, I think, do not so much reject Hebraic sensuality and embrace Neo-Platonic asceticism as fall for simple materialism, which ultimately leads us to treat both the universe at large and other persons in impersonal ways.

Taking a cue from you, I might recast the Seventh Commandment as follows: "You shall pursue the fullest possible union with your wife or husband, and through such union learn to enjoy union with God."

Chapter 8

Eighth Commandment

You shall not steal. (Exodus 20:13)

Rami: Before we go into the meaning of this verse, it might help to remember that we are following the Jewish verse numbers here. What Jewish Bibles see as Exodus 20:13, Christian Bibles see as Exodus 20:13–16. Same commandments, but it can get confusing if you are simply following chapter and verse.

Anyway, two things bothered my rabbinic predecessors regarding this commandment.

First, if the Eighth Commandment is just about stealing as ordinarily defined, why would God repeat Himself in Leviticus 19:11, "You shall not steal, you shall not deny falsely, and you shall not lie to one another"? Second, why list stealing in the same Ten Commandment verse as the prohibitions against murder and adultery? Murder and adultery are capital offenses that carry the death penalty. Stealing, however, is a much lower order of crime. And yet, there it is right alongside these two capital offenses. This must mean something, if we could only uncover the inner logic of the verse.

Let's look for the logic in Leviticus. The rabbis argued that linking stealing with denying falsely and lying makes perfect sense because people who steal will also deny that they did so, and then lie, even in court, in order to cover it up. So there is an intrinsic logic to God's linking stealing, denying falsely, and lying in Leviticus. If there is logic in Leviticus, there must be logic in Exodus, but what could it be? There can be only one answer: the Ten Commandments doesn't mean "stealing" at all!

Since murder and adultery, the two crimes linked to stealing in Exodus 20:13, are capital offenses, stealing, too, must be a capital offense. The only category of theft that carries the death penalty, however, is kidnapping. Hence, the Eighth Commandment should read, "You shall not kidnap" (*Sanhedrin* 86a). You can see how the Jewish mind, what we call *Yiddishe kup* (literally, "Jewish head") works: by taking matters literally, we are forced to take them metaphorically. For us, there is no distinction between the literal reading of the text and its metaphoric reading; the literal is the metaphoric. This allows us a lot of freedom in interpreting (or in many cases reinventing) text.

For the early rabbis, kidnapping referred not to the crime of holding a person for ransom, though that was not unknown, but to the crime of stealing a person and forcing him or her into slavery. It is actually slavery that the Eighth Commandment opposes! Too bad this rabbinic insight never made it into the King James Bible; we might have avoided centuries of oppression and a bloody Civil War.

Ancient rabbinic exegesis aside, and in no way discounting the link between stealing and kidnapping, most rabbis hold to the simpler view that the Eighth Commandment deals with thefts of all kinds: both theft of property and theft of one's good name, self-esteem, etc.

Mike: Thanks for outlining some of the ways rabbis dealt with the commandment. Apparently, your ancestors share a trait with some of mine: looking for patterns where no pattern may exist. To be fair, this seems to be a human trait. We're pattern makers and seekers. It's a useful thing most of the time. The flip side is that it may lead us to erect elaborate constructs where none are needed.

"You shall not steal." The best place to start is to take the commandment at face value. Don't take something that belongs to someone else. This is the most intergenerational of commandments, the one most readily understood regardless of one's age.

It's concrete. Don't take Susie's blanket, Mom's wallet, chewing gum from a store shelf. You can see that which tempts you! Others can as well. In fact, all the senses may become involved: sight, taste, touch, smell, and hearing. The prohibitions against idolatry, adultery, and even murder require, for most of us, a leap of imagination when first heard. "Don't steal," though, can be brought to life with something as simple as a purloined comb.

Our comprehension of the Eighth Commandment's range of application ought to expand over time. Stealing another's time, work, rightful place in a relationship, resources or opportunities—the commandment grows as we grow. Indeed, the commandment casts light on its fellow commandments. For example, idolatry might be considered a form of stealing from God. Murder is the ultimate act of theft against another human being, and so on.

Rami: I agree we tend to complicate things needlessly. I also agree that the commandment against stealing can be applied to the other commandments as well. Indeed, if we are going to say that we shouldn't take that which does not belong to us, we should also ask, "What does belong to us?"

The earth doesn't belong to me, but I to the earth. My body doesn't belong to me: indeed, there may be no "me" separate from my body. Even my thoughts and feelings aren't really mine. Most of "my" thoughts and feelings arise seemingly of their own accord, and I just notice them and then have to deal with them.

Along the same lines, everything I know I learned from someone else. I am obliged to say I have never had an original thought, though this fact does not preclude others—Isaiah, Buddha, St. Paul, and Einstein to name but four—from having them.

It is this aspect of "You shall not steal" that leads to the rabbinic mandate to honor your teachers by citing your sources. We see this all the time in the rabbinic literature where one rabbi speaks in the name of his teacher, often taking the older teaching in a new direction but never forgetting that his wisdom rests on that of his teachers.

This is the back story to Mark 7:28-29, "And when Jesus finished these sayings, the crowds were astonished at his teaching, for he taught them as one who had authority, and not as the scribes." Jesus spoke without reference to his teachers, whereas the scribes and Pharisees would always speak in the name of their teachers or the older prophets.

This has always troubled me. I have been told that Jesus spoke this way because his teachings were new, but as a student of first-century Judaism and having taught university courses in the historical Jesus, it is clear that while teachings *about* Jesus were new (though even here there seem to be parallels with, if not borrowings from, the religions of Greece and even Babylon), the teachings *of* Jesus were, by and large, not new. Jesus stood largely within Hillel's liberal wing of Pharisaic Judaism.

I understand that the Gospel writers sought to separate Jesus from his rabbis and from Judaism, and I have no problem believing that they simply left out Jesus' references to his teachers in order to strengthen their argument that Jesus was something new. But in my own mind, I still imagine him building his teaching on the foundation of his rabbis and honoring them by name as he did so.

This tradition of honoring our teachers takes a delightful twist at Hebrew Union College in Cincinnati, where the classroom podiums from which professors taught bore the names of those professors who taught there before them. The seminary was only a bit over one hundred years old, so there were not that many names, and one hundred years in a four thousand-year-old tradition is nothing, but I found it moving nonetheless.

Decades later, when I received the title "rebbe" from my Rebbe, Rabbi Zalman Schachter-Shalomi, he recited the names of his rabbinic lineage beginning with the Baal Shem Tov (1698–1760), the founder of Hasidic Judaism. The recitation followed the metaphor of a chain with each name being a new link. Reb Zalman added his name to the chain and then, in a moment that reduced me to tears, added mine as well.

None of us lives or thinks in isolation. We are all part of a lineage rooted in God. To take anything without permission, to use anything without giving thanks, is to violate the deepest meaning of the Eighth Commandment. When we truly understand the meaning of "You shall not steal," we realize that all we have—indeed all we are—is a gift from God. Humility, it seems to me, is the gift this commandment brings.

Mike: The story of the classroom podiums at Hebrew Union College is a classic. Certainly, humility requires us to acknowledge those (at least, all those we can identify) who have contributed to the development of our lives. We agree on this point.

All of the commandments assume and require acceptance of personal responsibility. In this case, I am responsible for my behavior with regard to theft, including such positive actions as acknowledging sources and debts. I'm struck by the commandment's starkness, by its "no excuses accepted" tone.

Taken seriously, the commandment pushes us to develop into a kind of person seldom encountered in "real life." Once again the matter of personal and community formation rears its head. The more I ponder the commandments, the more clearly I see that God envisions fashioning his people into a genuinely alternative community. The new community does not exist solely for its own sake, but for the sake of the rest of the world.

Think, for example, of the potential impact of a community that consistently strives not to steal from others. Suppose the Christian community (to pick on my own tradition) simply refused to use more than its share of the world's energy, water, land, and food resources. We probably would throw the economy into a tailspin, at least for a time. More to the point, we might free up resources for the poor. In addition, I suspect we would be taken more seriously by the world at large, both as a threat to vested interests and as a kind of good news to the poor.

Of course, following such a path requires us to lay aside our "normal" tendency to defend and protect "our way of life." Such a way of life, though, increasingly threatens the life of the planet and human life. It is becoming the way of death. The ancient wisdom embodied in the commandment turns out to be the kind of wisdom we need now.

Rami: This was very interesting, Mike, especially your idea of responsibility. I suspect many, if not most, of our readers will read your comments and think in terms of our responsibility toward the commandments: to keep or not to keep, that is the question. But I would like to suggest a deeper and more horrible responsibility: not responsibility *to* the commandments but responsibility *for* the commandments.

If, as I maintain, the Bible is a human document, then it is we humans who invented the Ten Commandments. It is we who said there is one God whose essence is found in the liberation of slaves. It is we who said that this God cannot be imaged (even as we imagined it). It is we who said don't murder, lie, steal, etc. But on what basis did we say these things? Were they just good ideas? And who is to define "good" for us?

So we placed these ideas in the mouth of God. Doing so was the ancient equivalent to Papal Infallibility. But if you aren't Catholic, Papal Infallibility is meaningless. Similarly, if you believe that God gave the Ten Commandments on Mount Sinai, the commandments God gave are inviolable. But if you don't believe that God gave them, then they are not really commands at all. It all depends on the story in which the commands are embedded, and the willingness of people to believe the story. It is the story, and not the commands themselves, that has the power. But only if we choose to give it power.

Even if we claim that God gave the Ten Commandments, our claim is rooted solely in our faith in the story that says so, which is little more than an assertion of one idea in the face of alternatives. A Jew might assert that God wrote the Hebrew Bible but not the New Testament. A Christian might assert that God inspired both, but not the Qur'an. A Muslim might assert God dictated the Qur'an but not the Vedas of the Hindus—and none of us have any proof of our assertions whatsoever. We simply assert, and sometimes insist, and, when we can get away with it, kill those who resist our assertions. But the simple, awesome, and horrible truth is that we invented all of it! It is our story. We just cannot stand this idea, so we run from it and do our best to close our ears to anyone who tries to tell us differently. Yet I think it is essential to our understanding of religion that we *own* our story.

The elements of the story are givens, but how you arrange them as well as the meanings you derive from them are yours. Since you own your story, you can change it. I would argue that is what psychotherapy is all about. We can't change the elements of the story, but we can change the story we create from them and the meanings we derive from the story. The task of the therapist is to help you reinvent your story.

My question is this: Can we drop the story altogether? I think that there are moments when the story drops away and we are radically, awesomely, fearsomely free. My own experience is that this freedom is spontaneous and temporary—an act of fierce grace from outside my egoic mind.

I would suggest that, if therapy is about learning how to create more healthy, fearless, loving stories, spirituality is about learning how to live, if only for a moment, without story altogether. I have had glimpses of this story-free liberation, and, while I believe it leaves one naturally just, kind, and humble, it doesn't allow for the creation of an ethical system. And since I cannot maintain that story-free life, I seek out ethical systems and the stories that sustain them.

I, too, need to hang my ethics on something greater, so, with equal lack of proof, I assert that there have been and continue to be spiritual geniuses among us who experience the absolute story-free non-duality of all life, and then translate that experience into a story that supports a personal and communal code of conduct designed to help us become more just, kind, and humble. The teachings of these rare geniuses are what Thomas Jefferson called the diamonds of wisdom buried in the dung of scriptural tribalism, xenophobia, misogyny, politics, and power plays. Our job as clergy is to liberate the diamonds from the dung, and align our lives and the lives of our communities with their wisdom.

The first step toward doing so is to recognize our responsibility for wisdom. There is no escaping it: we are the creators of our own story and the ethics they compel.

Mike: We differ, as we know well by now, over the ultimate source of the commandments. I do not believe we placed the words of the commandments in the mouth of God but, instead, that God inspired the words.

Insofar as I can discern, both of our positions on the matter are beyond conventional proof. In fact, both assumptions might be labeled faith statements.

All faith statements, including yours I think, place us in the uncomfortable position of dealing with competing faith claims. I see no way to eliminate the situation. What we do with it is another matter. We need not resort to violence, either to persuade others to accept our particular claims or to prevent others from embracing positions other than our own. Our personal and collective egos find this hard, but enough historical examples exist to prove it possible.

With reference to "responsibility," I believe myself responsible to the One in whom the commandments find their origins: to the One behind them, so to speak. In effect, the commandments are not only good for forming us into persons who worship God and build healthy community. A lifetime of putting them into practice may so condition us that we catch at least a glimpse of the living God and experience what life is like in God's presence. Even if such a thing does not occur, though, observing the commandments remains good for us and all those whom our conduct may affect.

As for "story," J. R. R. Tolkien's concept of man as sub-creator suffices. The Creator God spins the primary story, but as one created in the image of God, I may take the stuff of God's story and fashion my own. I cannot create the basic stuff of life, let alone life itself, but I can arrange and rearrange the ingredients. Indeed, I am responsible for doing so. By grace, God takes my efforts and weaves them into the greater story he is writing.

All of which, believe it or not, brings me back to "You shall not steal" and the previous postings. Given my perspective, it would be stealing to pretend I create anything per se. Everything is a gift from God. I may, though, become better skilled as a sub-creator and humble enough to take joy in the role.

Rami: Yes, we are both people of faith, meaning that we each have faith that we are right and the other is wrong, and lack incontrovertible proof to secure our argument. That's what makes this so much fun.

I don't think either one of us, however, is really uncomfortable with competing faith claims. In fact, knowing you as I do, it is our differences that make our conversations so enjoyable. I would also say that you are humble enough and brave enough to recognize that not knowing is the key to faith. At least speaking for myself, I revel in the philosophical freefall of not knowing. And I think you do as well. Violence is never an issue for people who love to dialogue. We don't need to convince one another of who is "really" right and who is "really" wrong (although we both know that I am really right, but, hey, I want to be humble too). I find little value in talking to someone who believes exactly as I do, or who parrots back to me what I am saying. I learn from you because you differ from me.

Case in point, I know next to nothing about Tolkien and was very interested in what you had to say about him. I would only add that when it comes to story the commandment should read, "You shall not plagiarize."

I'm only half joking.

Paraphrasing the Baal Shem Tov, the founder of Hasidic Judaism, "There is enough room in this world for everyone. The reason we feel so crowded is that we are trying to stand in someone else's place." Each of us has our own story, but somehow we come to believe that our story isn't as good as some other story, so we abandon our story for that other one. But the fit is awkward at best, and in so doing we are stealing from God's infinite diversity. As Eli Weisel once said, "God made humanity because God loves stories."

To bring this back to the Eighth Commandment: when we live someone else's story, we rob the world of our own. This was brought home to me ten or fifteen years ago. I was attending a Jewish educators' conference, and a middle-aged woman approached me for advice. She told me that she was the daughter of two Holocaust survivors, and that her parents lost all of their family in the Nazi slaughter. When she was born, her father was convinced she was the reincarnation of his sister. The woman was named after her deceased aunt and forced to live her aunt's story as best her father could remember it.

As you can imagine, she was miserable. She wanted to discover who she was, but she didn't want to dishonor her parents and violate the Fifth Commandment.

I asked her how old she was, and she told me she was almost 49. "This is wonderful," I said, "you're entering your personal Jubilee Year, from 49 to 50. Torah says that all debts are forgiven during the Jubilee Year, so for 49 years you honored your parents and your father's memory of his sister, but now that debt to the past is forgiven. Use the next year to begin to discover your true self, and continue that process for the next 49 years." She was genuinely relieved, though what she actually did, I don't know.

The seventeenth-century Hasidic rabbi, Susya of Hanipol, said, "When I die and stand before the Heavenly Judge, will I not be asked why I was not like Abraham or Moses? To such a question, I could provide a very convincing answer. No, when I die I will be asked only one question, the answer to which will determine whether or not I take my place in the World to Come, 'Why was I not Susya?' And to this I will have nothing to say at all."

Chapter 9

Ninth Commandment

You shall not bear false witness against your neighbor. (Exodus 20:13)

Rami: The simple meaning of the Ninth Commandment deals with swearing falsely in a courtroom. While it has other implications as well, let me start with this.

I mentioned earlier that the Ten Commandments don't cover all contingencies, only those that undermine the existence of society. This is clear with the Ninth Commandment. We learn in the Talmud (Sanhedrin 56a) about the Seven Laws of Noah that God imposes on all humankind. The seventh of these Seven requires the establishment of just courts. A legal system that is fair and honest is essential to a just society. So the rabbis spend a lot of time expounding the courtroom aspect of this commandment. Here are two examples:

First, even if you are convinced that a crime took place, you are prohibited from testifying that it happened unless you witnessed it yourself. This is true even if you were told that a crime took place by an unimpeachable source. Unless you witnessed the crime firsthand, you cannot testify.

The rabbis even prohibit what is a staple of TV crime drama: bluffing. Let's say there is only one eyewitness to a crime, but you accompany the eyewitness to court, thereby giving the impression that there are two eyewitnesses. Seeing the two witnesses and fearing conviction, the accused suddenly confesses to the crime and begs for leniency. While this may work on *Law & Order*, it is not allowed under Jewish law (Shavuot 31a).

In the *Mechilta*, an ancient rabbinic commentary on the book of Exodus, the rabbis link the Ninth Commandment with the Fourth Commandment, which deals with Shabbat. Since keeping the Sabbath witnesses to the truth of God as Creator (in the Exodus version of the commandments) and Liberator (in the Deuteronomy version), the theory goes that one who lies in court may also come to deny the existence of God and stop keeping the Sabbath, and in this way bear false witness regarding God.

I like this idea. To quote Mahatma Gandhi, "My life is my message." How you live attests to what you believe. This has always struck me as the best way to proselytize.

I attended a seminar once on how Christians can best proselytize Jews. We were taught to listen for openings in conversations. For example, if the Jewish person says, "Sometimes I feel so lost," we are to counter with, "Christ came specifically for the lost sheep of Israel. Let me tell you about Him." I never found this very compelling, and I said so during the seminar.

The teacher asked, "Well, then, what would move you to consider Jesus Christ as your Lord and Savior?" I said, "If I saw someone living a truly Christian life, a life devoted to loving God and loving one's neighbor without pride or prejudice, then I would be impressed. If I saw someone actually caring for the 'least of these' as Jesus put it (Matt 25:40), I would be drawn to ask this person his secret, and then he could tell me about Jesus. Nothing else would work for me."

Of course, I neglected to say that I know many wise and compassionate Christians who do live as Jesus intended and am still not compelled to convert, but I didn't want to be a total thorn in the presenter's side.

I suspect that the vast majority of people who call themselves religious are living lives that say something else; they are bearing false witness to the True God or bearing true witness to a false god. So this commandment has resonance far beyond the obvious.

Mike: I grant you the Ninth Commandment clearly applies to the courtroom setting. The examples you cite once again underscore the rabbis' concern for the protection of the accused as well as their determination to safeguard justice. Insofar as I can tell, a number of the "minor prophets" shared these concerns.

The commandment, though, predates both the rabbis and the prophets. The biblical text sets the giving of the commandments, including the Ninth Commandment, in the exodus journey. Regardless of what one may believe about historical accuracy, we are free to try to imagine how the commandment might have been heard in such a setting.

Perhaps, for example, it was heard in contrast to Egyptian practice of the period. While I don't know a great deal about ancient Egyptian law, I think we may reasonably assume that slaves were often subject to injustice. I rather doubt the Egyptian overlords of the Hebrews needed more than one witness to pass judgment on an Israelite (take, for example, the story of Joseph's imprisonment).

Imagine the Hebrews wandering through the wilderness. For the first time in generations, they must try to fashion a society, and the model most near to hand is that of Egypt. Would it not be ironic and sad beyond words if the liberated ones wound up imitating their oppressors? So perhaps the Ninth Commandment might be heard to say, "You shall not mimic the Egyptians and their brand of justice but shall instead adhere to a higher standard."

On a different note, I'm struck by an implication of the commandment: truth is required if justice is to be done. Frankly, our modern civil and criminal justice system often seems more concerned with achieving convictions, acquittals, or deals than with arriving at the truth of a matter. The justice system, it seems, is in danger of being taken over by the business model and its bottom-line mentality.

Finally, the commandment also carries personal implications. Again, try to imagine former slaves attempting to build a society. Questions of a justice system aside, bearing false witness against another would soon have led to quarreling and even blood feuds, tearing apart the group in short order. It's hard to bind yourself to your neighbor when your neighbor is libeling you!

Rami: While I appreciate the exercise of taking the Torah at face value, your suggestion that it would be "ironic and sad beyond words" if the Hebrews imitated the laws of their oppressors is itself ironic, for that may well be exactly what they did.

The Ten Commandments seem to borrow heavily from the *Egyptian Book of the Dead*, specifically the *Papyrus of Ani* (written around 1800 BCE), which, in chapter 125, offers a list of things a person must swear he or she did not do in order to enter the afterlife. The list includes "I did not engage in illicit sex, I did not murder, I did not rob, I did not lie, I did not curse God, I did not bear false witness, and I did not abandon my parents." Given the centrality of the *Book of the Dead* in Egyptian culture, and the fact that the Hebrews were enslaved in Egypt for centuries, it seems only natural that they would borrow from the Egyptians. The same thing happened with African slaves and Christianity in this country.

Borrowing from the dominant culture isn't a problem for me, and I can, to stick with your suggestion that we imagine the story as the Torah tells it, imagine God deliberately using the language, concepts, and forms familiar to the Hebrews when giving them the Ten Commandments. Indeed this might be hinted at in the opening word of the Decalogue, *Anokhi* (I), which is not Hebrew at all, but Egyptian.

The more interesting question for me is this: even with the borrowing, how do the Ten Commandments distinguish themselves from the *Papyrus Ani*? Two things come to mind immediately. First, the Ten Commandments are said to come from God, whereas the *Papyrus Ani* makes them a human confession before God. Second, the Ten Commandments contain no reference to an afterlife, whereas the *Egyptian Book of the Dead* is all about the afterlife, and chapter 125 is about how to gain entrance to it.

Despite (or maybe because of) living in a society obsessed with death and the afterlife, the Hebrews create a totally this-worldly religion, offering their Ten Commandments not as a means of gaining entry into heaven but as a means of creating a just and compassionate society on Earth. Compare the private death and secret burial of Moses (Deut 4:6) with the embalming and entombment of the pharaohs in the pyramids. This break with the dominant culture of death and afterlife is far more impressive to me than the natural borrowing from the *Book of the Dead*.

In fact, the more I think about this, the more impressive and important it seems to be. How did these people break free from the Egyptian culture of death? How did it not infect them? How is it that they didn't introduce a serious afterlife scenario into Judaism until the Babylonian exile in 586 BCE? If we want to point to something truly indicative of the God who says "choose life" (Deut 30:19) in the Torah and in Judaism, the this-worldly focus of the ancient Hebrews and their Jewish descendants may well be it.

I say this with some hesitation, however, because I find so much of Christianity diverging from Judaism and embracing the Egyptian obsession with death and the afterlife. This, to me, is the real irony and the real sadness.

My reading of Jesus is so life affirming and this-worldly—the kingdom of God is within you [or among you] (Luke 17:20-21)—and yet my experience of so many forms of Christianity is all about getting out of this world and into the next. I hope I am missing something here and would love to get your insight into this.

Mike: I ought to know better than to dangle that kind of bait in front of a world religions scholar! Borrowing forms, stories, language, and the like, of course, is not in dispute. That happens. My point was that it would have been a shame had the ancient Hebrews simply *copied* the Egyptians without altering or revising their system of law.

They, as you demonstrate, did not do so. Instead, the Hebrews did something creative. From my perspective, the Ninth Commandment is an example of that creativity: it provided protection for the accused, arguing that said protection included the weight of divine sanction. Viewed in this fashion, the Ninth Commandment becomes a piece of a larger way of life in which slaves, the poor, and the powerless potentially enjoy the same legal status and protections as the powerful. From there, it's not too far a conceptual leap to say that God takes the part of the underdogs of society. That was a revolutionary idea (and still is, more often than we care to admit).

I'm intrigued by your brief discussion of "this-world" versus "afterlife" centeredness. Christianity is not monolithic and never has been. In any given era, large numbers of Christians function out of a concern for the afterlife. Even in those cases, though, one finds a considerable emphasis on spiritual growth. When we unpack the written documents, we often find that "spiritual growth" implies learning to live in the present moment as if already in the presence of God (the classic definition of heaven). Good works, prayer, embracing joy, putting work and play and family into proper relationship, and a host of "worldly matters" assume great importance. One does not so much die and hope to go to heaven as one learns to follow the way of Christ and thus enter into "eternal life" in the here and now.

That being said, Christianity often veers in the direction you indicated. A few examples include sermons consistently focused on the potential terrors of the afterlife, human despair in the face of war and plague and the like, and the effects of mass-conversions-oriented revivalism. Sooner or later, though, the system self-corrects. In the past half-century or so, for instance, an increased appreciation of the Hebrew prophets coupled with a renewed sense of the "this-world emphasis" of Jesus has helped. The "emerging church" movement, in some measure, represents a recovery of this aspect of Jesus' intentions. You'll find the same kind of thing happening in many mainline denominations.

Personally, I find both emphases helpful. My strongest inclination is to deal with this life, to affirm it as a gift from God, and to seek to use it well (in accordance with the way of God). I also draw a kind of strength from the hope of a life beyond this life (from my perspective: resurrection and a new creation). It's not so much a hope for continued existence as it is a hope that evil shall not have the final word, whether with regard to the individual or the creation itself. To put it another way, I see my redemption and any redemptive act I may do as a minor foreshadowing of a greater, conclusive redemption wrought by God.

Rami: Your comments on this world and the afterlife were marvelous; I had no idea you were a Buddhist! *Samsara*, this world, is *Nirvana*, the world to come, if we are simply aware of it. We are always in the presence of God, or the *Shekhinah* as the rabbis call Her, but we are rarely aware of the fact. This is where spiritual practice comes in. I especially love *Practicing the Presence of God* by the seventeenth-century Carmelite monk, Brother Lawrence, and would like to hear your thoughts on the book.

Without going into any detail, my own practicing of the presence of God focuses on chanting various names of God found in the Jewish tradition. I find that the chanting of Names (these and others, including the Catholic *Hail Mary* and the Muslim *Ninety-Nine Names of God*) is a simple and profound way of opening my eyes, ears, heart, and mind to the presence of God in, with, and as all reality. In those rare moments when the "I" that chants realizes the "Thou" to whom it sings, and both awake to the singular YHVH that is all that is, there is a palpable sense of love, wonder, joy, grace, peace, and compassion that lasts . . . well, in my case, about three seconds. Still, it is a powerful three seconds.

You mentioned the emerging or emergent church, and I am a fan of this effort, as well as of the quest for the historical Jesus. I am drawn to Rabbi Jesus, my first-century cousin who, continuing and deepening the work of his teacher Hillel, recast Judaism in the image of compassion, but I wonder if in addition to recognizing how each era fashions an image of Jesus that mirrors its own hopes, needs, and prejudices, we also need to continually reclaim the Cosmic Christ, the Christ beyond Christianity and theology; the Son who, like His older Sister Chochma in the eighth chapter of Proverbs, calls us to the love-feast of God, a feast free from institutions, clergy, and the struggles for power and ideological purity that these always carry with them.

If I were to get back into the religious community business, I would open a coffee house rather than a synagogue. Our worship would be modeled on the Hasidic *farbregen*, a blend of singing, dancing, silence, sipping coffee or tea (the Hasidim drank vodka), and sinking our teeth not only into cakes and cookies but, more important, into the Wisdom that comes to us through all the great literatures of humankind.

Mike: I rather like Brother Lawrence's little book. His secret lay in his ability to focus on one thing: being open to the experience of God's presence, even as he went about the simple tasks of his typical day, such as washing pots and pans.

That's the ticket, isn't it? Whether making use of spiritual practices, such as the ones you note, or going about our daily chores, the trick is to learn to see the divine in the mundane. For me, that sense now comes most often as the result of a mental discipline, but it began long before I read or heard of spiritual exercises.

It came to me, initially, mostly through books. Three examples must suffice. As a small boy, I remember reading the Norse story of the death of the gods. The battle itself did not intrigue me, but the resolve of the gods to fight though they knew they must die did. In fact, the story took me out of myself for a few moments, and I knew I stood in the presence of One greater than myself.

Another breakthrough came when I read *The Lord of the Rings* while in the eighth grade. Gandalf's self-sacrifice on the bridge, when he falls into darkness along with his foe, the Balrog, broke through my deeply engrained reserve. For a few moments, I lay open, and One greater than myself touched my deepest heart.

In my freshman year of college, while sitting in a physics class and listening to a lecture, a sudden vision of the universe's integration struck me. I doubt the experience lasted more than three or four seconds, but for that instant I "saw" the big picture.

These, of course, are only examples gleaned from a larger group of experiences in my formative years. Later, I began to discipline myself to look at people, history, story, physics, the cosmos, and the like with eyes wide open. Sometimes I experience something similar to what you describe—not often, but sometimes. I find the occasional experience sufficient to sustain hope.

Chapter 10

Tenth Commandment

You shall not covet your neighbor's house, nor his wife, his manservant, his maidservant, nor his ox, nor his ass, nor anything that is your neighbor's. (Exodus 20:14)

Rami: The Tenth Commandment is different from all the rest.

In commandments one through nine, it is behavior that is prohibited; in this final commandment it is thoughts that are outlawed. How do you prohibit thoughts? There is a great deal we can say about this, but I don't want to overwhelm you or our readers, so let me offer just one comment now, and others as our conversation on the Tenth Commandment unfolds.

Let me start with one of the most innovative commentators on this commandment, Rabbi Abraham Ibn Ezra, a leading Spanish Jewish scholar (1093–1167). I am paraphrasing, but here is his three-part understanding of how the Tenth Commandment works:

First, recognize that the Torah is talking about your neighbors, people with whom you share a common socioeconomic status. You and your neighbor probably desire similar things, and if your neighbor has something you both desire, but that you do not yet possess, it is both normal and natural for you to covet it. Yet the Torah prohibits this. Since the Torah would not focus on something as natural as "keeping up with the Goldbergs," something else must be at issue here.

Second, Ibn Ezra said, imagine you are not talking about your neighbor but about the king (Ibn Ezra wrote in the time of the Spanish Crown). The king owns things way beyond your wildest dreams; however, because the king is so far above your "pay grade," you don't really covet what he possesses. You might covet your neighbor's ass, but owning the king's herds never crosses your mind.

Third, he said, now remember that you and your neighbor are the Image and Likeness of God, and being the Image and Likeness of God is greater than being king. So if you would not covet what is the king's, all the more you would not covet what is your neighbor's, given that you really believed your neighbor to be the Image and Likeness of God. But you do covet that which belongs to your neighbor! That can only mean that either you have forgotten that your neighbor is the Image and Likeness or God, or you deny that your neighbor is the Image and Likeness of God. In either case, you end up forgetting or denying God as well.

Following the logic of Ibn Ezra, we now see that the final commandment is the mirror image of the first. By coveting what belongs to your neighbor, you deny the reality of God. By denying the reality of God, you violate the First Commandment: I am YHVH your God.

The "cure" for covetousness is not to rein in your desires, but to regain your faith in the existence of God and humanity as the Image and Likeness of God.

I love the reasoning here. Another fine example of *Yiddishe kup*, the Jewish mind at work.

Mike: The Tenth Commandment's focus on thoughts poses a significant challenge. As you note, how can one control one's thoughts?

Perhaps "control" is not the best term. Try substituting "discipline." Is it possible to discipline one's thoughts or, along the same lines, to discipline one's feelings? Perhaps. Many of the classical spiritual disciplines are designed to reshape habits of the heart and mind so that we might more nearly focus on God or the good. This being so, I wonder if the Tenth Commandment might intentionally break new ground, serving almost as a teaser, saying in effect: "Oh, we're far from done just yet. By the time you get to me, you're just getting started."

Both my children are bright. They tend to catch on to new things quickly. Still, when they were very young, and I attempted to teach them how to relate well to others, I stressed actions. "Don't bite, hit, steal"—avoiding hurtful actions was the name of the game. As they grew, though, I shifted ground a bit. We could talk about the reasons behind our actions, why we do what we do. Guess what? Most of the time, we wound up talking about thoughts and feelings.

Of course, it's incredibly hard to discipline oneself. In fact, even the best among us falls far short of perfection. To quote Paul loosely, "We do not know sin until we hear 'you shall not covet.'"

To covet reduces us to a statement: "I want what he/she has; I must have it; I cannot be happy without it." When we see this in another, or read it in cold print, we may be able to discern its essential silliness. It's another matter when we are the one consumed by the desire.

You're right, Rami. There is more to discuss. After all, Jesus talked a good deal about thoughts and feelings. Many Christians understand the Christian life primarily in terms of coming to grips with the inner self, so that both our actions and our interior life play out in the sight and under the grace of God. All that—and we've not yet begun to discuss how to try to practice observing the commandment!

Rami: So much to talk about!

I am intrigued by your suggestion that the Ten Commandments is a spiritual discipline leading to the most difficult command of all: you shall not covet. As I think I mentioned months ago, I am taken with Jean-Yves Leloup's reading of the commandments as "you can live without" rather than "you shall not." Torah may be saying, "You can, with the proper discipline, live without coveting." But can we?

I agree with you, Mike, that there is no real need to distinguish between thoughts and feelings. Both are activities of the mind largely beyond our control. While I can choose to think about something in particular for a while, most of the time I just notice what my mind is already thinking about. As elusive as thoughts are, feelings are even more so.

Yet when it comes to coveting, however, there may be some nuanced difference between thoughts and feelings that does matter. Coveting begins as a feeling, a desire: "I want." But it only becomes true coveting when that feeling shifts into a thought: "and this is how I am going to get it." The feeling I suspect is primary. Without the desire, thoughts on how to achieve that desire would fade away.

Can I discipline my mind to put an end to coveting? I doubt I can stop the feeling from arising, since that seems to happen just below my consciousness. I only know I am desirous of something after the feeling is full blown. But I can, once thoughts begin to coalesce around the feeling, shut them down. Or at least shift my thinking to something else. But even this might still be a subtle way of feeding desire.

What if, rather than discipline the mind and its endless effervescence of thoughts and feelings, we simply observed the process itself? This is what the Buddhists call mindfulness, and we Jews call *hitbonenut*, contemplation or, more literally, self-observation. It is possible to watch the madness of desire without being moved to act for or against it. By simply noting the activity of the mind, you can allow the feelings to arise of their own accord and without moral import. By not judging or reacting to them in any way, you deprive them of the necessary mental energy to become complex thoughts of coveting; indeed, without added energy, they just dissipate.

The Tibetan Buddhists call this sky mind. You are the sky, and the clouds that form are thoughts and feelings. They may be pleasant or stormy, but they are never the sky. As long as you identify with the sky rather than the clouds, you need not control the weather; you need simply allow it to pass.

Mike: Perhaps the best response to the commandment involves a combination of our suggestions: discipline that results in reshaping habits of the heart/mind; shutting down covetous thoughts as soon as we detect them; defusing such thoughts by observing them in a detached manner. When it comes to handling dangerous matters, I tend to favor having more than one option.

I remember your fondness for Jean-Yves Leloup's suggestion that we translate the phrase "you shall not" as "you can live without." After reflection, I find myself with a problem. I'm not at all certain that "we can" fully actualize any of the Ten Commandments. On the other hand, observing them to the best of our ability will change us. In terms of the Ten Commandments, such a change involves becoming ever more devoted to God and more respectful of community-building boundaries.

Personally, I sometimes think of the Ten Commandments, including "you shall not covet," in mathematical terms: specifically infinity. We can never reach the end of the matter, we can never completely fulfill the commandments, but each improvement we make, each move toward fulfillment, is good in itself. Shifting to an analogy from physics, knowing we cannot achieve the speed of light does not negate the potential value of getting ever closer to it.

From my perspective, the commandments may also serve as needed reminders of our limits. The very fact that we cannot fully implement them introduces us to the complexity of our natures, including the tension between the image of God within us and what one might call our shadow side. The image of God within us is drawn to the commandments, wants to embrace and practice them, knows they represent in part what it means to be fully and healthily human. Something else in us, though, fears and hates the commandments. This shadow-self sees in them its potential demise, whether through elimination or transformation. And it fights back. With reference to the prohibition against coveting, it tries to dull our senses so that we fail to notice our thoughts and feelings and the way they affect what we do. Sometimes it turns bold and challenges the commandment itself, asserting, "greed is good" (to borrow a line from a mediocre movie).

When we pay attention to this kind of thing, we may get in touch with our own sinfulness, i.e., with the way we consistently fall "short of the mark." Such self-awareness may push us in any of several directions. We may try harder, or give up. Perhaps we will accept our limits yet continue to strive to fulfill the Ten Commandments. We may become more aware of God's grace, which frees us to undertake the living into the commandments secure in the surety of God's love even if we should fail.

Rami: I would like to make three comments in response, and then pick up on something you said earlier.

First, I think your point about never really living in full accord with these commandments is important and follows my earlier line of thinking. At the heart of all authentic spirituality must be a reality-based humility that recognizes our capacity for sin. The most dangerous person I can imagine is one who is "without sin." Jesus and his mother being exceptions, of course.

Second, like you, the ancient rabbis made a distinction between the image of God and the likeness of God. God intends to create humanity in both the Image and Likeness of God (Gen 1:26), but when the creation actually occurs, we are made only in God's image; likeness is left out (Gen 1:27). The rabbis taught that this means we are born with the capacity for godliness, the image of God, but that only our own will determines whether or not we actualize that capacity and thereby achieve the likeness of God.

Third, I agree that we must deal with the shadow-self. In fact, not dealing with it is one of the greatest failings of contemporary religion and new-age spirituality. We imagine all is light and love, that *we* are all light and love, but this is false and frightening. Our inability to accept our *Yetzer HaRah* (capacity for evil in Jewish terms) or our Fallen Nature (in Christian terms) leads to the projection of sin and evil onto others. The more we imagine God is totally good, the more we have to imagine a Devil who is totally evil. The more we imagine that we are totally good, the more we have to imagine an *other* (be it Jews, African Americans, Asians, homosexuals, liberals, conservatives, etc.) who is totally evil. This is the madness of binary theology that results in the religiously sanctioned violence that floods our daily news.

We need a more sophisticated understanding of God and nature, human and divine, which brings me back to your reference to Rabbi Saul/St. Paul. Paul says,

> While we were living in the flesh, our sinful passions, aroused by Torah, were at work in our members to bear fruit for death. . . . What then shall we say? That Torah is sin? By no means! Yet, if it had not been for Torah, I should not have known sin. I should not have known what it is to covet if Torah had not said "You shall not covet." But sin, finding opportunity in the commandment, wrought in me all kinds of covetousness. Apart from Torah, sin is dead. (Rom 7:5-8)

Compare Paul's teaching to that of Lao Tzu, the founder of Chinese Taoism. In the nineteenth chapter of the *Tao te Ching* (the "bible" of Taoism) Lao Tzu writes,

> Banish learning, discard knowledge, and people gain a hundredfold. / Banish benevolence, discard righteousness, and people return to duty and compassion. / Banish skill, discard profit; and there would be no more thieves. / Yet such remedies treat only symptoms so they are inadequate. One more is needed: / Reveal your naked Self, embrace your original nature, and ego dwindles and desire fades.

Lao Tzu and Paul agree that law and sin go together. They disagree, profoundly, over the implications of this connection. Lao Tzu says that law corrupts our true nature, and that if we would abandon law and take refuge in that nature we would return to our natural state of selflessness, duty, compassion, and simplicity. Paul seems to make the opposite claim, that our true nature is itself corrupt:

> So Torah is holy, and the commandment is holy and just and good. Did that which is good, then, bring death to me? By no means! It was sin, working death in me through what is good . . . . We know that Torah is spiritual but I am carnal, sold under sin . . . for I know that nothing good dwells within me, that is, in my flesh. (Rom 7:12-17)

Paul, if I understand him correctly, says Torah isn't sin, but the principles of Torah define sin and thereby make sin possible. This is true. If we didn't define speed limits on our highways, we wouldn't have people arrested for speeding. The law creates the outlaw.

More profoundly, however, Paul is also claiming, contra Lao Tzu and Judaism, that human nature is fundamentally sinful. The Pharisaic system in which Rabbi Saul and I were raised, and which St. Paul rejects, takes a middle position between Lao Tzu's faith in human nature and Paul's fear of it.

Where Paul seems to condemn the flesh and root evil in biology, his fellow rabbis, following the Torah, root evil not in the flesh but in the human imagination (Gen 6:5) and therefore articulate a more psychological approach to good and evil.

As I mentioned a few moments ago, people are created in the Image and Likeness of God. Because God has the capacity for good and evil (Isa 45:7), humans too have both capacities, which the rabbis call *Yetzer HaTov* (the capacity for selflessness and good) and *Yetzer HaRah* (the capacity for selfishness and evil). Both are necessary, and each must act to set limits on the other. An excess of either selflessness or selfishness can lead to societal breakdown. Society needs the creative interplay of egoism and altruism. The ideal, the rabbis taught, is to harness the egoic energy of *Yetzer HaRah* to the altruistic energy of *Yetzer HaTov* and in this way achieve true human fulfillment and holiness.

Mike: Let's start with your discussion of Paul.

I find your comparison of Paul and Lao Tzu interesting, and I agree it represents two very different approaches. Lao Tzu's approach, as you describe it, reminds us of the great myth of the "noble savage." If you recall, this myth posited that natural man (or woman) was uncorrupted until forced into contact with modern society.

Human experience teaches a different lesson: humanity is complex, a blend of the altruistic and nakedly self-interested. Insofar as I can tell, we have no reason to believe humans naturally practice selflessness, duty, compassion, and simplicity to the exclusion of greed, violence, and the like.

Paul argues that we are law-breakers. When we finally "see" the law, we become aware of our condition and our habitual practice of sin. To put it another way, we see that we are sinners because, well, we sin.

I think you may misunderstand Paul at one point. You write: ". . . where Paul seems to condemn the flesh and root evil in biology, his fellow rabbis, following the Torah, root evil not in the flesh but in the human imagination

(Gen 6:5) and therefore articulate a more psychological approach to good and evil." Paul uses the term "flesh" (*sarx*) to describe the totality of a human being: mind, body, spirit, imagination, or any other set of terms you may choose to use. Sin puts down roots in one's total being. Paul's understanding of good and evil is profoundly psychological. He can lament that while he sees and even wills the good, he may turn around only to find that he has done precisely the opposite. That's a fair description of the human situation!

It seems that Paul assumes *Yetzer HaTov* and *Yetzer HaRah*, but he also believes the fight is rigged in favor of *Yetzer HaRah*. Paul takes seriously the fallenness of society and concludes that we are corrupted by it long before we become responsible for our actions. He also assumes that "powers" are in play. Traditional Christian commentators describe those powers in terms of demonic forces; more contemporary scholars speak of the impersonal power of evil inherent in institutions and the like. Regardless of the particulars, Paul feels the deck is stacked against us when we are born and that the "house always wins." I find his viewpoint starkly realistic.

Paul's hope lies with God, particularly God as experienced in Jesus. Paul assigns both personal and cosmic significance to Christ, but the point to be made here is that the apostle finds in Jesus a kind of new life, a life that can challenge the power of sin and even defeat it.

The commandment "you shall not covet" triggered one of several transformations in Paul. For one thing, it forced him to abandon what seems to have been excessive confidence in human nature (or, at least, himself) in favor of a more realistic assessment of human potential.

Rami: I want to take a moment and make sure we make a distinction between the essentially colonial and racist notion of the Noble Savage and Jean-Jacques Rousseau's (1712–1778) idea of "natural man" with which it is often confused.

Rousseau, unlike Lao Tzu, did not trust in the goodness of human nature. Whereas the Taoist "natural man" follows the watercourse way of humility, patience, and *wei wu wei* (non-coercive action), Rousseau's "natural man" can be very violent and dangerous. Rousseau argues that concepts such as sin, wickedness, and lawlessness cannot apply to "natural man" because such terms only makes sense in an artificial society based on the imposition of law. On the other hand, and more closely parallel to Lao Tzu, Rousseau also argues that humans are driven by *amour de soi*, a positive self-love that society corrupts into *amour-propre*, pride. Pride, Rousseau says, leads to comparison, and both Rousseau and Lao Tzu argue that comparison leads to one-upmanship.

I believe the truth lies somewhere between the two philosophers' positions, though I think both Lao Tzu and Rousseau, as well as, from what you have said, Paul, are correct in arguing that there is something systemic to social constructs that leads us toward greed, violence, fear, etc. I take this to be what Paul means by "the powers."

With regard to these "powers," I am attracted to the teachings of Dr. Walter Wink, professor emeritus at Auburn Theological Seminary in New York City. In his book *The Powers That Be: Theology for a New Millennium*, he defines the powers as "the corporate personality or ethos of an institution or epoch" (27); "the impersonal spiritual realities at the center of institutional life" (28); and "the soul of systems" (29). For him, the powers are the "isms" and "ologies" that shape our thinking and our lives. Some of these powers can be positive, but many are evil. He sees Jesus as calling us to confront evil powers such as racism, sexism, materialism, consumerism, militarism, and the like.

Obviously, if we are called to confront these powers, we must have the capacity to do so successfully; otherwise the mission is futile and suicidal. Yet, as you said, the game is rigged. The House always wins, and the House is rarely on the side of the people. In Jesus' day, the House was Rome and the Temple aristocracy, and we know how that turned out. Even when Rome was rebranded as the Holy Roman Empire, and Judaism came under the sway of far more liberal rabbis, the House was still plagued by "powers" that fed off of and into human evil. Judaism, Christianity, and Islam hold out the hope that in the end God will win, but I am not so sure.

I do my best to stand up to the powers, but I do so without St. Julian of Norwich's conviction that "all shall be well, and all shall be well, and all manner of thing shall be well."

Mike: Thanks for the clarification with regard to "the noble savage." The distinctions you draw are on target. In my post, though, I had in mind a notion that enjoyed considerable popularity during the colonial period and even throughout a good bit of the nineteenth century. So our discussion has now identified three takes on "the noble savage."

I've always found Walter Wink's perspective on the powers persuasive and a fine lens through which to examine Paul's statements on the subject.

We may disagree on one matter, however. You state that if we are called to confront the powers, we must also have the capacity to do so successfully, else the entire thing is futile. If I'm overstating, feel free to correct me. From my perspective, and I think this would be true of Christian thinking as a whole, this is not necessarily the case.

I don't think it is too difficult to conceive of situations in which we might well be called to go up against a power beyond our strength to overcome. In such instances, we would be responsible to go as far as our wisdom and endurance allowed. At some point, the greater power would break or defeat us. We might truly be said to have failed. Yet it would be still right to try. My tradition teaches that such "failure" may actually lead to consequences that ultimately bring down the power in question, or at least set it back.

If you want an example of this kind of thinking, consider *The Lord of the Rings* (and, yes, you really need to read the book). Frodo, the hobbit, finally breaks under the pressure of the ring's power and his own suffering and so fails. His failed quest, though, has managed to bring the ring to the one spot where it might (just might) be unmade. At that point, things happen that are beyond his control or imagination, and his failure is redeemed by the destruction of the ring.

Rami: I think I overstated my position, and appreciate your reining me in. I agree with you that it is sometimes worthwhile to take action even when logic tells you that you are doomed to fail. There is something heroic in this, and, as you point out, you may trigger powers beyond your ken that shift things in the long run. I didn't mean to imply that one could know in advance that success was assured, but only that in some sense success was possible.

This makes me of think of God's teaching, "Be holy for I, *YHVH*, your God am holy" (Lev 19:2), and Jesus' saying, "You, therefore, must be perfect, as your heavenly Father is perfect" (Matt 5:48). If it is impossible for us to be holy and perfect, then demanding perfection of us is sadistic. So, as difficult as it may be to achieve holiness and perfection, it must in some way be doable even if the act of doing it necessitates the death of the egoic self.

If I remember correctly, what triggered all of this was the notion that the Tenth Commandment was the only one of the ten that deals with thought and desire rather than behavior. According to the nineteenth-century German rabbi Samson Raphael Hirsch, this detail, which makes the Tenth

Commandment unique, proves it is unmistakably the word of God. Rabbi Hirsch argues that while any flesh-and-blood lawgiver would think to prohibit blasphemy, murder, theft, and the like, only God would think to command us to purify our thoughts.

Not everyone goes in this direction, of course. In Judaism, we find intellectual consensus to be suspect; our pedagogical guideline is three Jews, five opinions. There is always a contrarian view. So here it is:

The ancient rabbis noted that the Hebrew verb for "covet" can also mean "to scheme after." They sight Exodus 34:24: "No man will covet your land when you go up to appear before YHVH, your God, three times a year." At issue is the fear that when I leave my land to go to Jerusalem to worship God during the three annual pilgrimage festivals (Pesach, Sukkot, and Shavuot), some unscrupulous fellow might seek to steal it from me. Hence they read the Tenth Commandment this way: "You shall not scheme to acquire your neighbor's household: his wife, his servants, his oxen, his ass, or anything else belonging to your neighbor."

This does away with our notion that the commandment seeks to regulate thought, and it makes all ten of the commandments purely behavioral.

One last observation before we wrap up our discussion of the Ten Commandments. The Exodus version we have been using differs from the version in Deuteronomy in a way the rabbis found significant.

The Exodus version of the Ten Commandments references your neighbor's house first and his wife second. In Deuteronomy, the wife is mentioned first, and the house second (Deut 5:18). According to the rabbis, the Exodus version refers to the nomadic life of Israel where owning a house was unthinkable, while Deuteronomy addresses the life of the Israelites after they have settled in the Promised Land and begun building permanent homes. God gave two versions for the two different situations in which the people would find themselves.

Mike: You're right. It would be sadistic to require something utterly beyond achievement unless the requirement being imposed had another purpose. Let's play with that idea for a moment.

Our problem, I think, is that most humans set the bar rather low. We're content at the personal level to avoid "excessive" sin. We, in effect, rewrite the commandments to fit us.

"Don't have too many gods other than the one God." "Don't lie excessively." "Don't steal enough to really hurt anyone else." On and on it goes.

Most humans and most societies have little use for "perfection," either as a goal or in practice. It's as if we decided to take up running each day for our health. Only, on the first day, we find out how hard it is to run at all. Each day thereafter we run or walk a little less. Finally, we reach the point where we do not run at all, though we keep our shoes and gear in a bag in the car.

The commandments, along with Jesus' injunction to be perfect, startle us. Someone dares to try to raise the bar. Frankly, he or they set the bar too high. However hard we try, we can't make the jump. We're not God, so we cannot be "perfect" as God is perfect.

The commandments and the injunction of Jesus (taken seriously) may force us to admit, "I'm only human." This, though, is not an admission of defeat but instead an acknowledgment of our true selves. We were never meant to be God. Humans were never created to be as God. We are made to be, well, human: the children of God. A great, self-imposed burden drops away. Strangely enough, acknowledging our legitimate limits frees us to rely on God for help, to pursue perfection without becoming paralyzed by our failures, and to get on with our core vocation of caring for the world and others.

Conclusion

Rami: We have come to the end of our text and our conversation, but as a gesture toward a conclusion, I think it might be interesting if each of us set forth a personal restating of the Ten Commandments. In my case I want to follow Leloup's and offer a more positive rendering of the commandments.

1. *God is the Source and Substance of all Being and Becoming.* Aware that the ego forever creates gods in its own image for its own profit, I recognize all ideas about God as products of human culture, bound by history and circumstance, and forever incapable of defining and describing the Reality Beyond Naming.

2. *God cannot be imagined and must not be imaged.* Aware of the suffering caused by allegiance to dogma and creed, I will live without making idols of ideas or mistaking any *ism* for What Is.

3. *Do not misuse religion or spirituality by taking God in vain.* Aware of the suffering caused by the misuse of God and religion in the quest of power, I will live without mistaking my path for *the Path*, my truth for *the Truth*, my idea of god for *God*.

4. *Remember the Sabbath and set it apart.* Aware of the suffering caused by unmindful living, I will cultivate the Sabbath as a weekly day of mindfulness, rest, and renewal.

5. *Honor your father and your mother.* Aware of the suffering caused by old age, illness, and death, I will care for my parents to the best of my ability and promote the honor and well-being of all elderly people.

6. *Do not murder.* Aware of the suffering caused by the wanton destruction of life, I will cultivate respect for and gentleness toward all life.

7. *Do not engage in sexual misconduct.* Aware of the suffering caused by sexual irresponsibility, I will uphold the holiness of sexuality by never degrading it through violence, ignorance, or deceit.

8. *Do not steal.* Aware of the suffering caused by exploitation, injustice, theft, and oppression, I will refrain from taking what is not mine.

9. *Do not lie.* Aware of the suffering caused by hurtful speech, I will speak truthfully and with compassion, avoiding gossip and slander, and refraining from uttering words that cause needless division or discord.

10. *Do not covet.* Aware of the suffering caused by unmindful consumption, I will eat, drink, and consume ethically and in a manner that is environmentally sound.

Mike: As I've already noted, I assume the commandments find their origin in God. They are not only good for us as individuals but also provide the basics of a healthy community. This means I may have less room than you to play with the core content of the commandments. On the other hand, the range of interpretation/application available to me remains rather wide.

I choose not to recast the commandments as vows, though I find your model intellectually stimulating. Rather, I prefer to regard the commandments as the high bar set by God for all individuals and communities, goals that challenge us to become far better than we have been, yet goals that may ultimately drive us to rest in the grace of God and accept our legitimate limits, even as we go on trying.

That being said, my personal wording of the Ten Commandments (following the order we've been using) would go as follows:

1. Dare to acknowledge a particular God as your Lord and God: the One who brought Israel out of Egypt and slavery. Remember, he is about the business of bringing you out of the narrow places, so don't be afraid to follow him into new insights, responsibilities and opportunities.

2. Never fall for the idea that you can capture God in a concept or an image—the moment you become aware you are doing so, stop it! Treat all concepts as partial and tentative, useful as tools but never settled or divine.

3. Never tie God's name to ungodly actions. Do not invoke God's name in the service of self-seeking, acquisition of power, feathering one's own nest, violence, or any of the other ills that plague humankind.

4. Observe the Sabbath that you may learn to remember, know, and rest in God.

5. Take care of your parents through acknowledgment, gentleness, and self-sacrificial service.

6. Never murder. When in doubt about debated matters, refrain from taking a life.

7. Be true to your spouse, in season and out, so that you may grow into the kind of person who loves steadfastly, even as does God.

8. Never steal. Start with particulars near to hand. Refrain from taking that which clearly belongs to your parents, siblings, or friends. The practice

will help free you from the tyranny of things. Grow so that in time you may learn to refrain from using more than your share of the community's or the world's resources.

9. Tell the truth. Do so humbly, knowing that your understanding of the truth may be flawed and need correction. Do so carefully, lest you hurt another needlessly. Tell yourself the truth about yourself, insofar as you can discern it, for that way lies freedom from lies and bondage. Listen to the truth about yourself when another speaks it.

10. Turn aside the desire to possess stuff. Such desire poisons relationships, leads to over-consumption, destroys the capacity to take joy in what we are given, and leads to community-destroying violence.

To tell the truth, I would add an Eleventh Commandment. It goes as follows: "Practice the commandments before the Lord your God as a child might play and work before his loving, trusted Parent; do not be afraid to try and fail, for God's love for you is a steadfast love."

Rami: At the heart of rabbinic Judaism is the notion that the reader co-creates the text with the author. While it may be that the Torah comes from God, its meaning comes from us. I am not inclined to take this literally. I don't think God writes books. But, as a metaphor, it is a very powerful insight.

There are some texts that come from the highest levels of human spiritual consciousness, pointing (given the limitations of the author's time, space, and cultural biases) directly to timeless principles that need to be applied in each generation. We have been dealing with one of these: the Ten Commandments. While the text speaks in a specific language to a specific people at a specific time, it also articulates timeless principles by which all peoples in all times can live effectively with love, compassion, and justice.

What made this project so rich for me, Mike, was having the opportunity to hear these commandments filtered through your heart and mind. If it is true that we co-create the texts we read by interpreting them in light of our own experience and knowledge (as well as our own ignorance and bias), then the pleasure I have found in reading these texts with you was in discovering your version of them.

When we started this project two years ago, I had no idea where it would take us, and I have been surprised by some of the avenues we have traveled together. I am also moved by how clearly our two voices emerged.

There is a consistency in our respective approaches that reflects the fundamental differences between our traditions, and yet suggests that no one way is sufficient. We balanced one another, I think, and did so in ways that enriched my understanding of the text and our traditions.

But there is something even more important to be gleaned from our conversation.

Interfaith dialogue is not new, but most of it takes place on the level of doctrine. Rarely do you find people of different faiths reading one another's holy books together. Granted, the Ten Commandments are no less a part of Christianity than they are of Judaism, but our traditions do understand them differently.

What I hope we have modeled here is a new avenue for interfaith conversation: trusted friends reading, wrestling with, and commenting on a sacred text. I would like to see this repeated over and over again with clergy and texts from as broad a religious spectrum as can be mustered.

It has been a blessing and an honor to work on this with you, Mike. What's next?

Mike: How could we have guessed or known where the conversation would take us until we held the conversation? The outcomes of a genuine conversation cannot be scripted ahead of time. The thing to do is to have the conversation!

Good conversations, especially those that stretch over long periods, are hard to come by these days. Truth be told, much within our culture discourages such endeavors. We opt instead for sound bites, shouting matches pretending to be discussions, posturing for the sake of core constituencies, and winning versus listening.

I'm grateful for a friend with whom I can hold a different kind of discourse. Like you, I hope we have modeled healthy interfaith conversation. Such conversation best occurs in the context of a deepening friendship, within which real differences and similarities may be discovered, and through which we learn to hear and appreciate one another's heart, mind, and heritage.

Have I mentioned laughter? Humor, both low and high, found its way into the conversation. I found this reassuring. In my experience, real conversation and relationships always involve humor, especially the kind in which we poke fun at ourselves. I learned a great deal from you, Rami. You gave me much to ponder as well. And, at times, you made me laugh.

As for what comes next, let's keep talking with and listening to one another and going where the conversation takes us.

Blessings on the journey behind us and the one ahead.

Bibliography

Daube, David. *The New Testament and Rabbinic Judaism.* Eugene OR: Wipf & Stock, 2011.

Eckhart, Meister. *Meister Eckhart: The Essential Sermons, Commentaries, Treatises and Defense* (Classics of Western Spirituality). Nawah NJ: Paulist Press, 1981.

Gödel, Kurt and Douglas Hofstadter. *Gödel, Escher, Bach: An Eternal Golden Braid.* New York: Basic Books, 1979.

Heschel, Abraham Joshua. *God in Search of Man.* New York: Farrar, Straus and Giroux, 1955.

Hirsch, Samson Raphael. *The Nineteen Letters of Ben Uziel.* New York: BiblioLife, 2009.

Jacobs, Louis. *Book of Jewish Belief.* New York: Behrman House, 1984.

Brother Lawrence. *The Practice the Presence of God.* New York: CosimoClassics, 2006.

Leloup, Jean-Yves. *The Gospel of Thomas: The Gnostic Wisdom of Jesus.* Rochester VT: Inner Traditions, 2005.

Schachter-Shalomi, Zalman. *Paradigm Shift.* New York: Jason Aronson, 2000.

Smith, Huston. *The World's Religions.* New York: HarperCollins, 1991.

Telushkin, Rabbi Hillel Joseph. *Hillel: If Not Now, When?* New York: Schocken Books, 2010.

Lao Tzu. *Tao Te Ching.* Gia-Fu Feng, trans. New York: Random House, 2011.

Wink, Walter. *The Powers That Be: Theology for a New Millennium.* New York: Random House, 1998.

For further reading

The Jewish Study Bible. New York: Jewish Publication Society, 2004.

Brettler, Marc Zvi. *How to Read the Jewish Bible.* New York: Oxford University Press, 2007.

Knight, Douglas, and Amy-Jill Levine. *The Meaning of the Bible: What the Jewish Scriptures and Christian Old Testament Can Teach Us.* New York: HarperOne, 2001.

Kugel, James L. *How to Read the Bible: A Guide to Scripture, Then and Now.* New York: Free Press, 2007.

Zornberg, Avivah. *The Particulars of Rapture: Reflections on Exodus.* New York: Schocken Books, 2011.

www.ingramcontent.com/pod-product-compliance
Lightning Source LLC
Chambersburg PA
CBHW072350090426
42741CB00012B/2996